ADELA

ADELA

The Noble Birth and Costly Death of Early Venture Capitalism in Latin America

JOSEPH JAMES BORGATTI

CHAPIN PUBLISHING

NEW YORK

Published by
Chapin Publishing
New York City, New York
info@chapinpublishing.com

Edited by Roberta Chase
Cover and design by Rick Hibberd
Cover portrait by Marcelo Montecino

Publisher's Cataloging-in-Publication Data

Names: Borgatti, Joseph James, 1923– author. | Train, John, 1928–
Title: ADELA:
The Noble Birth and Costly Death
of Early Venture Capitalism in Latin America

Joseph James Borgatti ; foreword by John Train.

Description: New York : Chapin Publishing, 2018.
Includes 1 chart. | Summary: The story of ADELA
(Atlantic Development Group for Latin America)
a corporation founded at the recommendation of the United Nations,
to underwrite private sector investments in Latin America.

Identifiers:
LCCN 2018951857
ISBN 9781732497405 (hardcover) | ISBN 9781732497412 (ebook)

Subjects:
LCSH: ADELA Investment Company–History. | Atlantic Community Development
Group for Latin America–History.
Development credit corporations–Latin America.
Investments, Foreign–Latin America. | Venture capital.
BISAC: BUSINESS & ECONOMICS / Corporate Finance / Venture Capital.
BUSINESS & ECONOMICS / International / Economics.
BUSINESS & ECONOMICS / Economic History.

Classification: LCC HG 5160.5.A35 B67 2018 (print)
LCC HG5160.5.A35 (ebook)
DDC 338.91

LC record available at https://lccn.loc.gov/2018951857

Printed in USA
First Edition

Printed on 100% PCW (Post Consumer Waste) paper
with FSC (Forest Stewardship Council) certification

To Sue and Elizabeth with Love.

Contents

꙳

ADELA

Foreword

><

ADELA wanted to show the world by a super-high profile example that you could make good money investing in Latin America, and to encourage others to follow: "Come on in, the water's fine!" Alas, what it showed instead was Train's Rule Four: Most things don't work. ADELA went bust.

Particularly, things don't work if the project is undertaken unrealistically, with an inadequate staff, and a defective corporate structure, attempting an exceedingly difficult task.

One thinks of the conquest of the South Pole: the businesslike Amundson, who took a whole year off to live among the Eskimos and learn sub-zero survival, who then traveled to the North Pole, and only after all this attacked the supreme challenge, the South Pole, with comparative ease. The heroic Scott, on the contrary, inadequately prepared, relied on good British grit to win through, but lost the race, his men and his life.

There was a great deal of amateurism in Adela. Many of the regional managers were attractive high-spirited young men who simply weren't experienced money-makers. It's hard to survive as a minority investor anywhere, but particularly in an unfamiliar territory with a tradition of commercial rascality.

I take a gloomier view than does the author of chief executive Ernst Keller. He was very skillful at jollying up the directors, but would give hell to a subordinate who departed from the party line by revealing that the ice was cracking. Similarly, I think the eminent consultants, Aurelio Peccei and the very wise Peter Drucker, should have been much more realistic, besides acting as cheerleaders for management.

Anyway, we are lucky that Joe Borgatti, probably the only person who could have written this book, and certainly the best qualified, has taken on the job.

Joe has had a prodigious experience of business life in many countries. He opened branches of Citibank in Latin America, developed a huge nickel mining and smelting complex in Guatemala, and has helped development banks resuscitate troubled deals from San Salvador to Egypt.

More recently he has been a hard-working board member of the Bulgarian American Enterprise fund, which has been phenomenally successful. In a word, he knows the subject from the inside and better than almost anyone.

So let us learn from this object lesson in noble failure!

JOHN TRAIN
14 Jan 2008

10

Acknowledgments

In writing this book I came to realize what Alan Bloom meant when he wrote: "The need to explain ourselves is irrepressible." I had been thinking for years about development and its disappointments. A late-in-life reengagement through the Bulgarian-American Enterprise Fund provided the chance to revisit the subject, but in a more detached way as a director rather than as a manager.

Family and friends provided help and encouragement, particularly my wife Elizabeth, son Steve, and daughter-in-law Roberta, plus friends (and colleague) Rafael Morales, Mary Kennedy Baumslag, and Ajay Mehra. Along with them were colleagues who made important contributions: Frank Bauer, Richard Boyle, Scott Falk, Fausto Garcia, Eduardo Garland, Peter Handscombe, Ernst Keller, Sherwood Kelley, Tom Mooney, Don Nicholson, Bob Ross, John Sanderson, Luis Valenzuela, and Doug Villepique.

A special word about John Train, whose own writing and encouragement inspired me to write this book. John thought I might have something to say about private sector investing for development, and he helped me immensely. Nevertheless, the book's limitations are my own.

And now, in Horatio's words:
Let me speak to the yet unknowing world
How these things came about.
(Shakespeare, Hamlet, act 5, scene 2)

JOE BORGATTI
New York City

11

1. How ADELA Came To Be

 ⤝

*Therefore I have called on all people of the hemisphere
to join in a new Alliance for Progress.*
—JOHN F. KENNEDY, MARCH 13, 1961

In the second half of the twentieth century, Latin American governments turned activist to induce growth. Into this era of large governmental economic development programs in 1961 came the granddaddy of them all, JFK's $100 billion Alliance for Progress for Latin America. This government-to-government assistance program held out large dollars for governments to reshape their economies and societies. But American Senator Jacob Javits had serious concerns about government encroachment on private activities. He also believed that Latin America would never achieve a satisfactory standard of living through governmental aid alone. His solution was to create a private-sector to private-sector economic development program for Latin America.

At the time, Javits was the longest-serving senator in U.S. history, twenty-four years. His was a progressive voice, which he used forcefully before a meeting of NATO parliamentarians in 1961 to argue that Latin America needed private capital from the industrialized world to grow. Their favorable response, and the enthusiastic alliance of another important U.S. senator, Hubert Humphrey, encouraged Javits to return to New York and recruit apostles. He enlisted George Moore, president of

Citibank (now Citigroup) and Pete Collado, EVP of Esso. Those two, with support from the Ford Foundation, began drumming up pledges from big banks and industries to create a new private vehicle for investment in Latin America. The argument for self-interest was compelling. For a modest investment, U.S. corporations would be able to offer a better alternative to socialism and statism. And they would improve their image with Latin governments, which might render discriminatory treatment, like expropriation, a little less likely.

The apostles attracted the participation of some fifty-five of America's largest enterprises. They included such powerhouses as IBM, Du-Pont, General Motors, Chrysler, U.S. Steel, and Caterpillar. Twenty-two were banks and financial houses, including Citibank, Bank of America, Fidelity, Loeb, Rhoades & Co., Wells Fargo, Mellon and Chemical Banks, but not the Rockefellers' Chase Manhattan. Why not? Did Chase and the Rockefellers want to withhold their knowledge and experience? After all, Chase President David Rockefeller was a leading international banker with special ties to Latin America from the time he had headed Chase's Latin American Division. Also, he organized and chaired the Council of the Americas and the Center for Inter-American Relations. Both institutions were working to maximize private enterprise contributions to the development of Latin America. In addition, he was chairman of the International Executive Service Corps, representing a stable of retired U.S. executives ready to go to Latin America, unsalaried, to help entrepreneurs with their business problems. Or could Chase's abstention be explained by Citibank's desire to deny prominence to Chase, which Citi was challenging in Latin America? Whatever the reason, Chase's exclusion deprived ADELA's founders of the benefit of much knowledge, experience, and Latin American connections, not to mention access to the experience of David's brother Nelson as political expert and private investor in Latin America. Nelson Rockefeller had been the U.S. coordinator of Inter-American Affairs, as well as assistant secretary of state for Latin America, and was twice sent to the region by U.S. presidents to report on conditions. Moreover, as a private investor, he had set up the International Basic Economy Corporation (IBEC), which pioneered a decade earlier what ADELA was being set up to do.

By 1963 Javits's NATO group was ready. It formed the Atlantic Community Development Group (ADELA) and established a working party to secure the initial capital. Two men in particular gave the group European clout, Giovanni Agnelli, chairman of Italy's Fiat, and Marcus Wallenberg, chairman of Sweden's Stockholms Enskildabank. The founders needed such important leaders to win over European businesses, which, initially, were reluctant. The German and British bankers, in particular, while not openly opposed, were less than enamored of associating with American business, knowing that Latin opinion was hostile to the United States. But at the same time they did not want to be left out of the club. So, many European corporations took minimum subscriptions. Finally, in January 1964, meeting in Paris, the group officially formed ADELA. Into it filed 54 American, German, Italian, British, Scandinavian, Japanese, and Latin American banks and industries (eventually 240 shareholders in all), mainly giant firms, who put in $16 million of capital. Yet, missing were French investors, even though ADELA was formed on their soil.

Was this another across-the-Atlantic misunderstanding? Or were the French simply not buying the American optimism on which ADELA was based? Were the Americans seeing a solution where the French saw a problem in Latin anti-Americanism? Possibly the French, from their own history in Haiti, were sensitive to the bad feelings created by the repeated American interventions in Latin American states. They were surely aware of outspoken Marine Corps General Smedley Butler's public boasts: "I was a racketeer, a gangster for capitalism. I helped make Mexico and especially Tampico safe for American oil interests in 1914. I helped make Haiti and Cuba a decent place for the National City Bank boys to collect revenues in." One French business leader expressed his own contrary view of joining ADELA as "hooking the small European carriages to the powerful United States locomotive which will pull all of us into the wild jungles of Latin America." And so, for all those reasons, the French stayed out of ADELA (although two French companies did come in later).

But in trying, futilely, to allay French and others' fears of U.S. domination, ADELA's founders embedded a fatal defect: a stipulation that no one company could hold more than a $500,000 investment. That guaranteed that no one would have a significant interest in ADELA to protect. What was everybody's would turn out to be nobody's, just when ADELA would need somebody to lead it.

2. The Climate for Investment
in Latin America in the Sixties

In the early 1960s, ADELA's founders could read in the *Wall Street Journal* that Latin America had "vast unmet business needs." The region was experiencing the world's highest population growth rate, while local capital was forming too slowly to provide sufficient investment. In recognition, Latin governments were becoming receptive to foreign private investment. The founders could easily sense opportunity.

But political risk loomed also. Fidel Castro's overthrow of the Cuban government at the end of the '50s ushered in a long decade of political change. Since independence in the nineteenth century, conflict had threatened the old regimes. Now, the tension was greatly heightened by public clamoring of students and *campesinos* (farm workers). Responding to Che Guevara's advocacy of revolution, they were staging political disturbances all over the region. In reaction came a wave of military takeovers, which heightened an already disturbing trend toward statism. Moreover, as fast as Alliance for Progress dollars were flowing in, local capital was fleeing. Was it after all so propitious for venture capitalism to be going into Latin America?

Moreover, Latin America was a bear of a place to embrace. The region, including the Caribbean countries, contained almost three times the area of the United States. Consider the task of covering this territory in the '60s, when jet plane service within the region was in its infancy and modern telecommunication was almost a generation away. A further complication was the Andes mountain range bisecting South America for 4,500 miles from north to south. In fact, trade or transport routes had never connected the Latin American nations even though all but two, Paraguay and Bolivia, faced the shores of great connecting seas, the Atlantic, Pacific, and Caribbean. Actually, their trade routes were not with each other but with the developed nations in North America and Europe.

Latin American countries shared only one common experience: they were once American colonies. The French bestowed the generic term "Latin America" in their 1862 occupation of Mexico. Possibly by invoking Latin roots, as with French-speaking Quebec and Haiti, this conveyed some legitimacy to the deed. But the name was somewhat of a misnomer. Several of the countries were English-speaking. More than one third of the people in the rest spoke Portuguese—a Latin-based tongue, like Spanish, but alien to most Spanish speakers. And in the 17 of the 31 countries that spoke Spanish, it was not always the language of the majority—which could be Quechua, Aymara, Garifuna, Kekchi, Kaqchiquel, or other Indian/Mayan tongues.

Even more daunting than diversity of language and territorial extent was that the countries represented such differing states of development. It was one matter for ADELA to invest $3 million in a tile manufacturing operation in a suburb of industrial São Paulo, Brazil, a metropolis of more than ten million people, with a strong technology base and vibrant stock exchange for exiting the investment. Another matter was investing $3 million to grow rice in rural, low-lying British Honduras (now Belize), an undeveloped, yet-to-become nation of some 100,000 people, with a per capita annual income of barely $1,000 and rudimentary infrastructure services, where devastating hurricanes occasionally blew sea waters twenty miles inland, right up to ADELA's rice farm. If only the enterprises could have been switched! They knew how to make tiles in Belize, but next to nothing about growing rice or exporting it. Worse still, that government, in a vestige of British colonialism, handled rice sales through a government marketing board. But in Brazil they knew a lot about rice growing. And farmers marketed their own products to a large consuming public.

The farther from ADELA's home base in Peru, and the less developed the service infrastructure and local market, the more problematic it was to make an investment viable. Not to mention the problem of providing the follow-on monitoring and nurturing that every new project needs. ADELA did establish regional offices to cut travel and increase local familiarity. But, in doing so, it traded off a loosening of supervisory controls and in doing so reduced access to the experience and skills that were available at headquarters in Lima.

And what about local capital moving out as statism was advancing? In 1964, the year ADELA was born, a *New York Times* editorial warned that private capital had become disenchanted with Latin America, "where the investment climate has been clouded by inflation and hostility to foreign enterprise." Early in 1965, the *Economist* questioned what ADELA could achieve in this "highly unsuitable setting, where capital has a tendency to disappear without a trace in the quicksand of inflation." Evidently, local capital caught on, if ADELA did not. In the early '60s, John Crow wrote in his *Epic of Latin America* that for every dollar that was going into Latin America, a dollar and a half was coming out as native capital in flight. Meanwhile, ADELA's owners and managers seemed unconcerned that they were putting money in as the locals were taking theirs out. Why didn't anyone do a political and currency risk assessment? In his book *Famous Financial Fiascos,* my friend John Train, former shareholder and director of ADELA, investment advisor, and the author of some twenty books, categorized ADELA as "folly recurring endlessly." He wrote: "One blithely embarks on projects in faraway lands that one would shun at home where one understood the hazards."

My former employer, the International Nickel Company (INCO) of

Canada, in contrast, approached its first overseas investments in Latin America (Guatemala) by packing off its senior management and several directors to a weekend seminar away from the office. Under the tutelage of a Columbia University professor and a senior executive from the Inter-American Development Bank, the group considered the cultural, political, and other important differences to be encountered and ways for accommodating them. It provided INCO a frame of reference for mounting its new venture in Guatemala.

ADELA's founders seemed to need no help in understanding the environment in which ADELA would operate. Confident in themselves and their ability to manage whatever risks they would encounter, those corporate chieftains would not have paused to reflect on John Train's observation that "distance lends enchantment to the view." Walter Wriston, then in charge of Citibank's enormously successful overseas division, would boast: "We have this huge branch network in Latin America that makes money year in, year out. We've been remitting profits from Brazil every year through this whole mess. That's what everybody who beats us up over cross-border doesn't realize, and we're not about to put it on the broad tape either." But, as Wriston's words imply, that kind of acquired wisdom was kept in house and not passed on to the executives who set up and managed ADELA.

Wriston didn't mention that Citibank had developed a business model that gave its managers a solid start for setting up operations in foreign climes. Managers would lead off (with help from the home office) by securing a piece of the banking business of the multinational companies that Citi was already serving elsewhere around the world. Then they would go for the accounts of upper-tier local corporations by offering to handle their business with the same efficient systems and products developed for their multinational customers. A manager setting up a new shop would be trained and guided by this model and would be fortified with two thick and well-thumbed manuals: *Accounting & Procedures* (known throughout the region by Citi staff as *La Biblia*, or the bible) and *Credit Policy & Routine*. Relying on these two experience-based guides and on a few key staff who knew the local territory, a manager could fairly quickly develop a client base and bring a branch operation to profitable status at low risk, while getting to know the place and the people.

But ADELA's investment managers weren't getting this kind of help, even though their business was more complex and they were very green. Venture investing, which implies being locked in for the longer term, often with no built-in exit, was a lot more risky than the short-term lending that commercial banks practiced. Moreover, many of ADELA's projects were developmental, such as resorts, farming, and real estate, which would require years to pay off. Meanwhile, they needed to understand the local environment if they were to manage the risks.

The Latin American sphere was layered like an onion. The outer layer was a thick barrier to entrepreneurial achievement in the form of a stultifying mercantilism that Spain had introduced when it conquered much of Latin America. That system was based on state control over economic production. Moreover it viewed the economic system not as expandable but as a zero-sum game in which one firm or nation's gain was another's loss.

Mercantilism's traveling companion was the heavy-handed bureaucracy brought from France, Spain, and Portugal. Only in Brazil did an imaginative people develop an antidote, the *jeito*, which involved finding ways around any restrictions. The Brazilian people became quite clever at dodging their system's many obstacles and barriers.

The onion's under layer was the economic burden of servicing the debt resulting from huge government borrowing abroad to finance state-sponsored industrialization. For some countries the interest charge consumed a third of their income. The resultant inflation and currency devaluation might have been mitigated if the industries had been productive and export-oriented. But that did not happen.

Peeling the onion further revealed policies to protect local industries that often had an anti-foreign capital bias, or more precisely, as Daniel Patrick Moynihan, America's ambassador to the United Nations described it, anti-American. Those policies included currency controls as well as nationalization of foreign investment. ADELA's founding director, Pete Collado, executive vice-president of Esso gained firsthand experience, as his own company's holdings were nationalized in Peru in 1968, when Army General Juan Velasco Alvarado seized power in a military coup, and in Venezuela in 1974. On becoming interim president of ADELA in 1975 Pete had to move ADELA's headquarters first from Peru to Venezuela and then to the United States because his persona had become non grata in those two countries.

The state-directed economy had become the post-World War II paradigm for development. Argentine economist Dr. Raul Prebisch preached so-called "structuralism" from his pulpit at the United Nations Economic Commission for Latin America and the Caribbean (ECLA). The idea was that commodities export had failed to provide for development because the industrialized world sent back manufactured exports at high prices. The antidote was import substitution industries, an idea that Latin governments eagerly adopted. Big ideas, explains my scholar son, like hemlines, tend to move to extremes, until a backlash sets in. The theme of the time was centralization in politics and economics, the hallmarks of communism and socialism. Interestingly, when this book was first conceived, the pendulum had swung to decentralization.

What stood in the way of Latin America's economic growth the most was the politics. Land tenure had been concentrated in a few hands since colonial times. Meanwhile, the region's population had mushroomed as two trends converged – high birth rates and declining death rates: 62 million people in the beginning of the twentieth century grew to 200 million by mid-century and 500 million by its end. Per capita incomes failed to keep pace because of unsuccessful economic policies and bad government. In that situation the few haves found themselves fighting a rear guard action to keep the status quo through repressive government against the many and increasing have-nots. Unsurprisingly, the revolutionary winds from Castro's Cuba were fanning popular ardor to redistribute land. Political and social tensions were high.

Adding to the volatility of the Latin American sociopolitical scene was the United States' very active and possibly destabilizing role, intervening in Latin America at least thirty times in the first thirty years of the twentieth century. Following World War II, in which the United States had been less than solicitous of regional sovereignties in its pursuit of Axis collaborators, it began a new round of interventions. First was a heavy-handed ouster of the Arbenz regime in Guatemala in 1954, which was followed by civil war. In the '60s came the Bay of Pigs and other U.S. attempts to overthrow the Cuban regime. A U.S.-backed military coup in Brazil led to an anticommunist purge and the establishment of a military dictatorship. The '60s also saw the Marines dispatched to the Dominican Republic to quell factional fighting. In Panama, resentment led to anti-U.S. rioting and a break in diplomatic relations, leading to a renunciation of the Panama Canal Treaty. In 1973, the U.S. campaign to destabilize the government of Chilean President Allende culminated in a bloody military coup. Later in the '70s and through the '80s, the United States was back in Nicaragua, with the Contras to force out the Sandinistas.

So, were the circumstances really so propitious for U.S.-style venture capitalism in Latin America? Or did the French, after all, have reason for their standoffishness toward ADELA? At a minimum, ADELA's navigation plan would have to steer in a sea murky with regulation and bureaucracy, between the Scylla of a vast and diverse territory and the Charybdis of social and political turmoil as well as economic discrimination.

3. The Entrepreneurial, Capitalist-Led Approach to Economic Development, Plus an Aside on Development's Sad History

༷

I began this book with Schumpeter's notion of the entrepreneur as the engine of economic growth. Harvard Business School Professor Tarun Khanna has aptly described this innovator, who introduces new products and new processes for producing them, as "somebody who is exercising productive mutiny against some status quo."

Latin America had such entrepreneurs. The region's "informal economies" were chock-a-block with entrepreneurs hustling to make it. Hernando de Soto's seminal work *El Otro Sendero* (The Other Path) making the case for legitimizing the informal sector had not yet appeared. But informal economies were well demonstrated in markets from Mexico City to Lima to Buenos Aires. The entrepreneur's role was more significant in the less-developed economies because the local oligarchies, which controlled much of the wealth, weren't doing much innovating; they were just trying to conserve their positions.

Introducing capitalist funding and investment experience to entrepreneurs' ideas and drive could produce all kinds of new ventures to spark economies. ADELA had those resources—the cash to invest plus the business know-how and market access represented in its roster of shareholders. And, as economist Jeffrey Sachs wrote, "Capitalist-led development works almost everywhere."

The other necessary ingredient for sparking an economy—along with the entrepreneur backed by capital and big-brothering—is a minimum of honest, able government. The trio can jump-start economic activity and introduce an opportunism that can be catchy. Turning that into solid, *sustainable development* (words sacred to the development community) depends, the pundits say, on getting the political and economic institutions right, and then letting private enterprise flourish. A single example of how it works was Ireland's Celtic Tiger of the 1990s, which showed an amazing economic growth rate. A takeoff on *Asian Tiger*, referring to the economic growth of Asian nations such as Taiwan, *Celtic Tiger* was used to describe Ireland's economy over a decade of rapid economic growth between 1995 and 2007. Ned Kelly, a friend who was part of the team that structured the Irish miracle, described it to me while he was on loan to the Nicaraguan government in the 1990s as it attempted to reverse ten years of Sandinista misrule. Sadly, his voice, though lyric as an Irish tenor, was lost in the cacophony of advisory voices telling Violeta Chamorro's new government what to do.

The Asian Tiger bloc offers an interesting regional comparison with Latin America. By 1965, when ADELA started, the average per capita income in Latin America was almost twice that of the nations to be called Asian Tigers. But while Latin American nations chose state-led development, the Tigers freed their economies, gave export incentives, and then followed a development path that made Japan, Singapore, South Korea, and Taiwan economic powerhouses. By the early 2000s their real per capita income was about two and one-half times that of Latin America's. Unfortunately, among the Latin countries, only Chile followed the Asian example. The others preferred to finance their development by debt, mainly public, rather than by private investment.

The dean of a Central American university once told me that when you are searching to grow your economy, you look around and see what works and what doesn't, and you choose what does. That is what the "Chicago boys" in Chile did. President Pinochet gave those Chilean economists, who had studied economics at the University of Chicago, a relatively free hand to implement economic reforms, including deregulation and privatization. Chile became Latin America's best economic success story by following the free market economic model of the Asian Tigers. The Chicago boys failed the first time, but they reoriented their policies around economic reform and free trade, which sent Chile on the long road to economic growth continuing to this day. Thus, on opposite rims of the Pacific, successful economic development was based on market economics and relatively good and uncorrupt governments. I am mindful that those countries also had strong authoritative hands at the helm (hence the "boys" were given a second chance to get it right) and some judicious help from the state.

But when government leads not by trying to create conditions for development but by trying to predetermine the winners, it devolves into wasted resources, negative development, and cynicism about the process. Yet many Latin nations tried to force and control the development process by creating government-developed financial institutions that decide which projects to finance. Their landscapes became littered with the shells of abandoned development banks owning thousands of bad projects. I worked as a consultant on privatization for one Central American country that had created four government-development institutions: an industrial development bank, another for forestry and wood, a third for agricultural development, and finally one just for bananas, with nowhere near enough investment management, talent, and probity to go around. The four used heavy USAID and other donor funding to invest about $500 million in some one hundred companies. A few firms that received large loans or equity investment simply never started up. Many others were closed down, while still others were taken over and "managed" by the four development institutions. "Managed" meant, in effect, dissipating the assets.

Capitalist-led approaches, with government involvement limited to providing the capital base, have had interesting and varied success.

Three are useful in discussing the ADELA case (four with the smaller LAAD, which I describe in Chapter 4). Two are multilateral agencies: the International Finance Corporation (IFC), operating world-wide, and the Inter-American Investment Corporation (IIC), operating in Latin America and the Caribbean. The IFC belongs to the 180-member countries of the World Bank Group, and the IIC belongs to the 43-member countries of the Inter-American Development Bank group. The U.S. Government-sponsored Enterprise Funds, which the U.S. Congress established in the early 1990s to promote democratic and free market transitions in the former communist countries of central and Eastern Europe, represent the third approach. All three entities are privately managed but publicly funded, either directly or indirectly. Major differences in their operations and effectiveness stem from the amount of government involvement in their operations. Government shareholders select IFC/IIC directors, who can be political appointees with little or no investment knowledge or experience. Directors may change as administrations change and thus cannot generally provide independent, experienced private management. Enterprise Fund directors are mainly retired executives and venture capitalists. Keeping their appointments separate from politics has been an important reason for their success.

The three capitalist approaches have all fared well. But their contributions to economic development are difficult to define. A former U.S. assistant director of the IFC during the ADELA era concluded: "The IFC is going to have a difficult time making much of an impact in developing countries...as long as it sticks to relatively risk-less ventures." Financial circles often commented that although the IFC was dedicated to the private sector, more and more it was financing big business that the markets could have handled.

A thoughtful friend at the Inter-American Investment Company (IIC), which operates throughout Latin America and the Caribbean, described its program in this way: "The companies we lend to are small and medium-sized, as opposed to the large companies that the IFC lends to. We lost a lot of money in the early days by taking significant risks with companies: a lot of start-ups, a lot of 'dream' projects. So, between 1989 and 2001, I would argue that we were risk-takers, and had the poor results to show for it. Since the Argentine crisis of 2001/02 we have radically reduced our appetite for risk and have cut back drastically on financing through equity (very few new participations in equity funds), and have tended to fund normal operations rather than 'projects.' Consequently, we have had some good earnings for the last couple of years, which means that we have partially improved the accumulated losses we had until 2002." Funding "normal operations" suggests to me that the IIC was taking a piece of the existing lending pie, not enlarging it by funding the new entrepreneur.

The Enterprise Funds have represented a more imaginative variation of the entrepreneurial, capitalist-led approach to development. The American Congress, through the the SEED Act (Support for Eastern European Democracy), provided funding for Enterprise Funds in many Eastern European countries, from Albania to Russia. Applying public monies to spur private sector development might have failed but for the strategy of turning the capital over to private management under volunteer (unpaid), veteran oversight. After receiving one-shot funding, the Enterprise Funds could use their best judgment as to which risks to take. They became venture investors entering newly independent societies somewhat as capitalism's advance parties to fund small business in the nascent private sector. Focusing on a single country, they could give it their full attention, as contrasted with the global IFC and the regional IIC.

The Enterprise Funds have produced impressive results, even allowing for the usual quota of failures in venture investing. Most of them have emerged some fifteen years later, after contributing substantially to economic development, able to return capital to the U.S. Government and still have considerable funds left for starting legacy foundations in their respective countries. Here follows a review of one, the Bulgarian-American Enterprise Fund, with which I was associated for 20 years until its liquidation in 2015. The review was written for presentation at the 65th reunion of my graduate school class in 2012.

"A Beacon of Integrity"
The Bulgarian-American Enterprise Fund

Once in a while a big idea avoids the black hole down which foreign aid seems to disappear. One big idea was the creation of Enterprise Funds to invigorate the economies of the former members of the Soviet bloc. In the early 90's, as communism crashed, the U.S. Congress passed the SEED Act to establish venture investment entities (Enterprise Funds) in the ten former Soviet republics. They were publicly funded (it was yet too risky to attract private investment) but privately managed by volunteer (read unpaid), independent boards. This was capitalist-led development at its more adventurist.

Usually foreign aid goes out once and that's it. But the Enterprise Fund money went out, got paid back, and was recycled to businesses again and still again. And when their 15-year mandate was up, while two of the ten had failed, which is about par for the course in venture investing, the Enterprise Funds had 41% more in capital than they had started with. In the process, they had created thousands of jobs and enterprises, developed the products and institutions of the modern financial market, such as mortgages and stock exchanges, and set a standard for correct corporate behavior. The U.S. Government took back half the original capital and permitted the Funds to use the remaining money to endow legacy foundations in their respective nations to further their development as modern European democracies.

Results of The Enterprise Funds

	(in millions of $)	
	Started with	*Ended with*
The U.S. Russia Investment Fund (TUSRIF)	329	316
Polish-American Enterprise Fund (PAEF)	255	352
Ukraine & Moldova (WNISEF)	150	125
Central Asian-American Enterprise Fund (CAAEF)	106	15
Hungarian-American Enterprise Fund (HAEF)	73	32
Czech and Slovak-American Enterprise Fund	65	10
Romanian-American Enterprise Fund (RAEF)	61	142
Bulgarian-American Enterprise Fund (BAEF)	58	431
Baltic-American Enterprise Fund (BalAEF)	50	50
Albanian-American Enterprise Fund	301	83
Totals:	1,177	1,656

This is the story of one of the Enterprise Funds, the Bulgarian-American Enterprise Fund (BAEF), on whose board the same 10 directors sat for some 17 years. The Polish Fund is held as having produced the most dramatic results. They started with $255 million in a market of 38 million people that had already experienced capitalism; and they ended up with $352 million for a gain of 38%. Great! But the Bulgarian fund started with $58 million in the European Union's poorest country —a market of barely 7.5 million people that had never known capitalism—and finished with over $400 million, for a gain of 800%. The Fund didn't just make a ton of money, it made a reputation as people to be trusted who had made a positive difference in a lot of lives. The Bulgarian-American Enterprise Fund and its bank, the Bulgarian-American Credit Bank, became a beacon of integrity in a sea of corruption.

Bulgaria in the 1990s was a tough place to do investing. After 50 years of communism, it had everything to learn about capitalism and democracy. Meanwhile, the old communists were taking what they could get, corruption had come to be a way of life (Bulgaria earned a rating of the most corrupt country in the 27-nation EU), and democratic government was toddling. By the middle of the decade the strains would bring an economic as well as political meltdown—with inflation reaching 1,000% in 1997, and banks collapsing all around.

It was bumpy sledding for the BAEF. Its first three investments went sour for some $3 million, perhaps not so unusual in a business where the lemons tend to ripen first. But this was followed by the loss of some $500,000 when loan payments remitted by farmer clients disappeared within the banking system. The Central Bank President's response to our complaint was to suggest starting our own bank. All this was happening amid tensions with USAID representatives who were pushing us to put more money more quickly out the door through equity investments. Also, as a major distraction, the BAEF was hit by a $20 million lawsuit from an important Washington-based figure claiming breach of contract and defamation of character in connection with a real estate development project. That suit would last 5 years until it was finally decided in our favor by the U.S. Supreme Court. Imagine what a diversion those events presented, and what they did to morale during BAEF's initial decade.

All of this was reported in a 1996 Wall Street Journal article headlined "U.S. AID'S BOONDOGGLE IN BULGARIA." The article called us "troubled," citing our recent negative annual rates of return of -169% and -40%, and classed us as one of the worst performers among the Enterprise Funds. We were said to be incurring excessive costs in the U.S., bleeding dollars while our executives lived well, drawing big salaries in comfortable offices on the American side of the ocean, spending more money in Chicago than in Bulgaria, and not drawing Bulgarians into our operations. The article concluded that the U.S. Congress should take a really hard look at its handiwork. Separately, an AID audit found us to be greatly overstaffed and unlikely to become profitable.

But the BAEF persevered and came back. We stopped listening

to the bureaucrats and altered our strategy away from equity investing into secured financing. And by then, having gained a knowledge of the local environment, we turned opportunistic. With the banking system in trouble in 1996, we perceived a need for 5-10 year financing among small enterprises whom no one was financing. Therefore, we took the Central Bank President at his word and started a bank of our own. The opportunity had come about because the 35 banks in the country, mostly subsidiaries of European banks plus a branch of Citibank, were not doing much local lending. They felt safer buying Euro government bonds with the depositors' money. So we took the plunge, even though only one in our group had actual bank experience, and he had been away from banking for some 30 years.

Another opportunity turned up in the country's ski and sea resorts that needed to upgrade for tourism. We started by financing mom & pops in the mountains to add a room or two to become bed and breakfasts; in the process we learned how to get equity-type returns on our loans. With this acquired experience, we moved to the Black Sea beaches which were attracting tourists from Germany, Russia and Britain. What we offered, which no one else was doing, was to provide financing to the managements of the aging communist-built hotels on the Black Sea to privatize and then to refurbish them. Eventually we did some 250 such transactions, becoming the bankers to the hotel sector.

From day one, our bank, BACB (Bulgarian-American Credit Bank) was "different." It shunned the so-called "conglomerates" (read corporations) and concentrated on lending to the SMEs (small-medium enterprises). The bank did not go after deposits but funded itself through buying money wholesale in the market, whether from European banks, European aid agencies or the aforementioned IFC (International Finance Company, part of the World Bank), and of course our own BAEF. This unique funding model allowed the BACB to match the maturities of the money borrowed to those of the money lent, which was generally for periods of five or more years.

The BACB's game, in the words of its CEO, was making calculated judgments about <u>people</u>. It came to know its clients well and to know the businesses they were in. It differed from the typical commercial banks because it did one thing and did it well: make a collateralized loan of five to ten years' maturity. This strategy became viable through a process of careful selection of staff and wise mentoring with the aid of directors. The bank introduced mortgage lending, but not so much for homes. Some 70% of its mortgage loans were business loans to SMEs. BACB developed great expertise in client screening and loan structuring, but also in close supervision of loans and timely restructuring. And when necessary, the bank also tapped into the real estate expertise built up in the BAEF.

The BACB came to earn ratings by agencies, within and without Bulgaria, year after year, for a decade, as the most profitable bank, the best managed, etc. When, as part of our wind-down, BAEF sold the bank, it went for a record price.

The BAEF, meanwhile, was not just lending to builders and promoters, but also developing properties itself through a property management subsidiary, Bulgarian-American Property Management, which was constructing and selling office buildings, apartments, homes, shopping centers, even a gated community. At the same time, BAEF/BAPM was helping to create the other financial products and institutions of a free market economy such as pension funds and REITs, plus special-purpose vehicles containing packages of our secured loans that offered interesting yields to pension funds and other investors. Management also built a profitable leasing company, which it later sold off for a large gain (48% IRR).

By now, you should be wondering how on earth all of this came about, given our awful start and the state of things in Bulgaria. There were three reasons for the group's success: capital (money and people), strategy and leadership.

Although one study said that BAEF had too little capital to be self-supporting, it seemed about the right amount of money to get something good going. And experience showed that we could hire good, young, if underprepared people. That latter condition was remedied by providing training on the job and making advanced education in business available to all. The result was that 77% of the staff came to hold master's degrees in business. In order to hold on to those good people, including the CEO, without whom this story could not have been written, the board came up with a long-term incentive program that paid to the employees 20% of the gain on the sale of any investment. The plan was administered by the Audit Committee of the Board, which determined who got what percentage based on the employee's relative contribution to the achievement of the gain. (For the generality of bank employees, there was a bonus plan which rose with each year's profits; in our last year of ownership, the bonus reached 10 months' salary.) It was the American Capitalist system where people are rewarded for merit: the better you do, the more you get. The staff had to wait almost 15 years for much of their reward. But it was worth the wait, for the total gain that was spread among 3 dozen participants came to be almost $100 million. Incidentally, after the U.S. Congress had approved the plan, many of the other Enterprise Funds adopted it. Understandably, we experienced little turnover in either the Fund or the Bank during the 15 years. So capital resources, especially in the form of people, was an important factor in our success.

As for strategy, it took 4-5 years to get it right. We needed to understand Bulgaria and come to terms with the environment before we could develop a business model that fit the place and times. The strategy of innovatively financing the smaller entrepreneur through secured lending at term was a winner that became more doable as conditions began improving. That happened because the pull of being able to qualify for entrance into the European Common Market forced Bulgaria to take measures that brought a certain political and financial stability.

But it was leadership that carried us through the bad patches into our great years and was the determining factor. It was the leadership of a CEO who persevered and led us back from a losing situation. He worked with his people to develop their effectiveness, was willing to scrap what didn't work for what could, saw where to go, and innovated to get there. Perhaps this is not so surprising when you learn that this man, who had agreed to give the job a try for a few years and stayed on for 19, was a product of Harvard Business School and McKinsey, as well as the Vietnam war, where he was an infantry company commander.

It was also leadership by the Chair that ensured full debate of issues (the mark of a great board). More than once a member has remarked: "Best board I ever served on." The Chair achieved an activism where board members applied their particular skills and experiences to help develop opportunities or solve problems working with the staff (see attached Addenda). And it was the Chair who went to Washington to win congressional approval of the incentive plan.

As mentioned earlier, The U.S. Government allowed us to use the $400+ million gained from our venture in Bulgaria to endow a foundation in that country. Our mission is to help Bulgaria develop its private sector and become a modern European democracy. We have brought over from the Fund and the Bank the same systems and procedures for working with people who get money from us plus the same CEO and Board, and a few staffers, including our chief operating officer. To enhance this group we have added a few very key professionals from outside our universe. To date, we have approved some $108 million in 332 grants distributed in six areas: Art & Culture, Agriculture, Archeology & Tourism, Civil Society, The Economically Disadvantaged, and Education & Libraries. Early reports plus our own feel, suggest that the foundation is on the way to making a positive difference in the social and political life of the country.

Returning to ADELA

There was one private-sector development initiative that pioneered in Latin America what ADELA would try to do, and had already invested $157 million in thirty-three Latin American countries by the time AD-ELA got going. In 1949, Nelson Rockefeller set up his International Basic Economy Corporation (IBEC). Backed by $45 million in loans from Chase Manhattan, IBEC had enjoyed some notable successes. But it faced numerous problems in Latin America, including hyper-inflation in Brazil and hostility in Venezuela. Along the way it also ac-quired unproductive and marginal facilities. Eventually, by the time it folded in the 1980s, IBEC had lost millions through ventures in which it had no expertise. I have wondered why ADELA did not school itself on the IBEC experience.

ADELA's initial approach was like that of the Enterprise Funds in the sense of being quite entrepreneurial. In Central America, for exam-ple, ADELA established some projects that significantly contributed to regional development. First, ADELA's man found the right project and then assembled the necessary mix of partners to make it go: local entre-preneurs, know-how associates from abroad, and capital-strong public development banks armed with public policy clout. Because the part-ners were comfortable with ADELA's man, he could structure a minor-ity shareholding for ADELA that still allowed it to exercise leadership as an internal peacekeeper. With this formula, ADELA invested profitably in a few projects in Central America, the most notable of which was the development of a complex of chemical companies in Nicaragua.

But too often ADELA played the dual roles of entrepreneur and in-vestment manager, for which it was unsuited, while it should have been helping local entrepreneurs to develop their own projects. Bad examples abound and not just in Central America: cattle fattening in Venezuela, rice farming in Belize, resort development in the Dominican Republic and Brazil, a sugar-alcohol complex in northern Brazil, real estate development in Central America and Argentina, and shipbuilding in Peru, to mention a few. Why ADELA departed from its original game plan is the story of this book.

An Aside on Development's Sad History

Capitalist-led development has been shunned generally in much of the world that needed it most, Africa and Latin America. Those regions have favored the state-led variety, which has failed. In the more than fifty years since World War II, the world's governments have spent in the trillions of present-day dollars in development assistance. Yet Africa and parts of Latin America, the places receiving the most aid, remain deeply poor and stagnant. "Human beings have trashed the joint," as Kurt Vonnegut once said about the state of the world. Two years after his death in 2007, the *Wall Street Journal* reported that the world would soon reach a record one billion hungry people, roughly one in seven humans on the planet.

U.S. Senator Jacob Javits wrote in his autobiography: "Despite all the effort and money expended in development aid in the past thirty years, we have not succeeded in significantly narrowing the gap between rich nations and poor." Indeed, United Nations studies have shown that 70 out of 100 countries that have received development aid for decades have declined economically. At the turn of the century, incomes for almost half of them remained less than they were in 1970, thirty years earlier. USAID actually admitted that much of the investment that it and other donors financed between 1960 and 1980 "disappeared without a trace." Maybe there was a trace: the heavy indebtedness of the third world.

The U.S. Alliance for Progress, right in America's backyard, generally failed to meet its goals: the Latin nations failed to make the needed reforms, especially in land tenure. After Kennedy, American presidents lost interest, and the $22 billion spent, while huge, didn't go far in meeting Latin needs. Speaking of American foreign aid, former President Clinton told a philanthropic conference, "about half our foreign aid never leaves these shores." Undaunted, a few years ago, governments of the industrialized nations including the United States–goaded by Irish rock star Bono–raised their annual contribution from the $60 billion annual average to $100 billion. But Bono at least exhibited better sense than aid administrators have shown: he wanted aid to be conditioned on need and proven capacity to use it effectively.

Yet a strong popular presumption persists that the developed nations can bring about economic development through foreign aid, a notion nourished by bureaucrats and other interested parties whom Graham Hancock, of the *Economist*, called the "Lords of Poverty." He wrote:

> In tribal society it is dexterous dodging of the real issues that allows the rainmakers to stay in business even though they don't make rain; likewise, in Western public-spending, the same tricks of trade ensure that huge sums of our money continue to be transferred to aid organizations that seldom–if ever–produce any tangible results.

Foreign aid's true believers, who must fill platoons, remain convinced that it "ought to work" and can work if they are in charge. They carry on like the legendary bureaucrat: having lost their way, they redouble their efforts.

Foreign aid touches guilt feelings in industrialized nations, where citizens can be persuaded to feel some historical responsibility for the state of things, which helps to explain why critics of foreign aid have fared poorly and why so many national leaders have ignored major dissidents. Lord Bauer, the great development economist, earned disdain when he described foreign aid as the process by which money is taken from poor people in rich countries and given to rich people in poor countries. More than disdain greeted William Easterly, a senior economist at the World Bank, when in 2001 he publicly criticized the bank's record of helping underdeveloped countries, arguing that their development programs had misapplied Western growth models to least-developed countries (LDCs) that had different economic, political, and cultural circumstances. He was promptly fired.

Peruvian novelist and Nobel Laureate Mario Vargas Llosa railed against northern "cultural imperialists" who "cultivate a good conscience for themselves." His son Álvaro, a noted political commentator on international affairs, used his Latin American Perfect Idiot character to say "We're poor. It's their fault." The idiot species, he wrote, bears responsibility for Latin America's underdevelopment. Its beliefs—revolution, economic nationalism, hatred of the United States, faith in the government as an agent of social justice, a passion for strongman rule over the rule of law— derives, in his opinion, from an inferiority complex.

Whatever the popular misapprehensions, among both north and south, leading thinkers have argued rationally, if futilely, that development aid does not work. Nobel Prize winner Milton Friedman and Lord Peter Bauer have powerfully argued and demonstrated its failure, and have described foreign aid as "inter-government subsidies." Econometric studies showing that aid fails to affect the speed of development have further supported their arguments. The mass of studies and plethora of thinking have generated two strong arguments against official foreign aid: it creates a sense of dependency and gives bad leaders time to postpone reforms that would bring prosperity. Arvind Subramanian, in *A Farewell to Alms*, further emphasized that foreign aid damages economic governance and competitiveness.

Two other arguments help to explain why the trillions spent on aid have failed to produce growth. Corruption is widely reported to be endemic among recipients. More difficult to control is that one dollar of aid is indistinguishable from any other dollar in the government till, making aid easy to plunder. Second, foreign aid has been, as experts show, over-politicized. Politics and policy, it is believed, are too strongly linked even for the typical conditionality of aid to sunder.

Nevertheless, to rule out all foreign aid would be to also eliminate good and needed assistance. It would be better to separate state-led developmental aid from humanitarian aid, which focuses on relief from natural disasters or conflicts and probably should have been intensified long ago and channeled through NGOs. Competition among them could then work for timely, effective delivery of help. Heavyweight philanthro-capitalist sponsors such as Bill Gates are now making this a real possibility. My feeling is that developmental aid, government-to-government, deserves its bad name and should be buried along with the assumption that provides its sustenance—that foreign aid and revolution are the only cures for poverty.

What has been shown to be effective is capitalist-led development, which works by helping entrepreneurs develop businesses. This, I believe, is the thrust of Prof. Sachs's thinking when he argues that capitalist-led development works anywhere, and it is in line with the views of Dean Glenn Hubbard, Columbia Business School, who has proposed reforming foreign aid to concentrate on business funding. Countries would win this aid by instituting economic reforms that facilitate start-ups and business expansions. The basic requirements for such a program, I believe, would be minimally honest and effective government, more than minimal care for the rule of law, economic reform toward a market-driven economy, and stimuli for the entrepreneur.

4. How **ADELA** Invested its Money

༽ᡣᡄ

ADELA's game plan was venture investing: buy blocks of shares, usually minority holdings, in young businesses. This form of investing had been developed for new, small enterprises with big gain or loss potentials and no access to bank loans. As ADELA was starting up, the *Economist* expressed its doubts:

> ADELA hopes to become the catalyst for private investment in South America. It's a unique institution using ... the sophisticated tool of the investment trust in a highly unsuitable setting, where capital has a tendency to disappear without trace in the quicksands of inflation. It remains to be seen what it will achieve.

In the early '60s, venture investing was still uniquely American, like basketball, not yet internationalized. I was in business school in the 1950s when Professor Georges Doriot founded America's first venture capital fund, the American Research and Development Company, out of which came the Digital Equipment Company, among others. Then Arthur Rock, one of his students, went on to become a pioneering venture capitalist who helped form numerous start-ups, including Intel Corporation and Apple Computer. But it would take some years before Europe and Latin America would become familiar with venture investing. An exception to prove the rule, coincidentally, was classmate Philippe

Allain. As ADELA was forming, he was starting Brazil's first supermarket, PegPag (literally, "pick and pay"), which he later sold handsomely to a multinational. Those who remember the French reluctance to join ADELA will have noticed that Doriot and Allain were French.

Equity investing was risky, even in the United States. It required bringing in some big winners to cover the inevitable losses on the several others. The *Economist* reported that nine of ten venture-capitalized businesses fail, and that it could be ten years after start-up before the original investors could get their money from an investment. Meanwhile, investors would earn no dividends because the venture investment companies would have to keep reinvesting cash to finance growth. Therefore, they would need a strong capital base and tight control of overhead to avoid running out of money. Managers had to be skilled at spotting and vetting good new deals and guiding them through the early stages. This also required knowing something about the businesses being invested in. Finally, the managers had to know when to cut lost causes and avoid sending good money after bad.

Investing in the developing world of Latin America presented additional challenges. The investors had to mitigate currency risks by funding businesses that exported in hard currencies. On occasion, they would need to bring in state-owned investing agencies as shareholders to insure against political and economic discrimination. Simple concepts, but complicated to execute. The venture investor would need to have a voice as a minority investor and be respected in corporate councils, although that was not the norm in that part of the world. Enterprises in Latin America were closely held, and sales to outsiders were not the rule. ADELA's manager in Argentina, Eduardo Garland argued: "It made no sense to be minority shareholders in Latin America where most companies were family-owned. Minorities had no leverage or legal protection for their shares and no secondary market to get rid of them." He might have added, as one cynical friend did, that by issuing shares an enterprise can obtain money from foreigners without having to pay them back. In contrast to a loan or bond, a share certificate contains no promise.

My colleague Len Harlan, a major private equity investor, echoed from his vast experience: "The easiest thing is to invest; the difficult thing is to get out." Given the paucity of developed capital markets that could provide exit through IPOs (initial public offerings), the investor would have to work up imaginative alternative exit strategies. Few countries in Latin America had well-developed stock exchanges where shareholdings in local companies could be sold.

Finally, because investors must spend so much time with the companies they invested in, they needed to finance just a few at a time and to specialize in particular types of businesses rather than diversify. For ADELA to invest in any number and type of ventures all over Latin America before conditions were right and the company was ready was, as I have suggested, a major challenge.

Nelson Rockefeller, with the aid of the family bank Chase Manhattan, tried equity investing through IBEC before and during the ADELA era and failed. Then a group of American banks, led by the same Chase, created the Libra Consortium Bank in London to pool the funds of various banks for lending to Latin America. That institution also folded. Foreign bank lending, until very recently, had not regained the leading role it held in the 1970s. In fact, after the region's debt crisis in the '80s, foreign private financial institutions became scarce in Latin America. Among American banks with branches around the territory, Citibank had the field practically to itself. Citi's branches, it seems, had been able to adapt to their environments.

If the Rockefellers couldn't make it in Latin America, their own backyard, either with equity investments or loans, and big banks couldn't do it as straight lenders, what chance was there for a fund using a business model based mainly on equity investing with some lending—often to the same party? ADELA's business model was to buy minority shareholding

45

in a new company, help it develop, and then sell out and proceed to another investment. "New" meant a "greenfield" enterprise in a new kind of activity. But with the first blush of experience, ADELA had to loosen that tight rule to permit investing in existing businesses that were seeking to expand. Then the rule was relaxed further to allow lending to the enterprises as well as investing in their shares. Even with those adjustments it was questionable whether the equity-based model could make it in the Latin American environment, or in any other emerging market. The two other ADELAs, one for Africa (SIFIDA) and Asia (PICA), also inspired by Senator Javits, closed their doors in the '90s. Their strategies, too, had been equity-based.

What seemed right for ADELA were the big projects, like pulp and paper in Brazil. ADELA acted as the catalyst to match a strong Brazilian group that knew the local side of the business with big foreign partners who were in the same line and who could provide access to foreign markets. The vibrant São Paulo stock market provided an exit mechanism for the foreign partners. Having brought the right parties together in the right market, ADELA could then itself invest, which it did for $3 million in shares and profited handsomely when the shares were sold. Another successful project followed in São Paulo, possibly ADELA's biggest gain. ADELA invested $1.5 million in equity for a 25 percent stake in the Alpargatas Shoe Company and realized a capital gain of almost $5 million when it sold to an investors' pool formed through a large Brazilian banking institution.

But big projects could be disastrous when ADELA went in as a principal rather than as catalyst for other participants. The rice farm in British Honduras, described later, comes to mind. Possibly the most egregious was Paraty, a resort condo development in Brazil. In a 1980 review of ADELA's condition, the International Finance Corporation (IFC), a commercial subsidiary of the World Bank, commented that Paraty contained all the problems that later caused ADELA to become

46

insolvent. Among the criticisms: the site was too far away to adequately oversee; ADELA knew nothing about the business; no mechanism existed for outside project reviews and cross checks; and the company was unwilling to cut losses early on.

The Paraty Resort development project in Brazil

Paraty is a resort town that lies around the middle of the 325 mile coastline between Rio de Janeiro and São Paulo. Dating to 1531, this colonial town is a well-preserved national historic monument. In the 1970s, tourism rediscovered its breathtaking coastline and beautiful beaches; it seemed to be a developer's dream.

In 1972, ADELA, Brascan (formerly involved in the development of Brazilian utilities and now a holding company in Canada), and two Brazilian institutions—a financial conglomerate and a publishing company—joined forces to purchase six thousand acres of beachfront property close to the town, intending to develop it for tourism. One part of the area (1,400 hectares or 3,460 acres) called Laranjeiras, was developed as a condo project. In 1976, ADELA acquired the remaining 1,100 hectares (2,718 acres) separately, and it became the Trindade project, a badly executed real estate speculation that resulted in a total loss.

Early on, mishaps assailed the Paraty project, including the pullout of the two Brazilian partners. Nevertheless, the two foreign partners, ADELA and Brascan, carried on. Construction began in 1974 and soon faced infrastructure cost overruns on the club building, tennis courts, pool apartments, golf course, and, most especially, on the building of an eight-kilometer access road. Sales of units were jeopardized when Brazil was hit by the oil crisis and gasoline sales were banned on Sundays. This meant that potential buyers could not make the five-hour weekend drive from São Paulo. Moreover, Brazil's economy fell deep into recession. By 1978 the project had consumed more than $20 million against an original budget of $10 million and was stopped. ADELA's original 1972 investment of $250,000 had ballooned to $13 million.

About small project development funding

For ADELA to fund the smaller, often newer firms that were the vast majority of their clients, ADELA needed a different approach than making equity investments. Conventional wisdom in the '60s, and for some time afterward, held that for development financing to succeed, entrepreneurs must be provided with permanent equity capital rather than saddled with loans they must repay. From the start, ADELA followed that wisdom in funding most of its clients. But other voices contended that whether entrepreneurs were funded by loans or equity, their cash flow and productivity were the keys to success. Theoretical backing came from Franco Modigliani and Merton Miller, who won a Nobel in economics for demonstrating that whether firms are financed largely by stock or debt, they are worth the same. Which is better depends on factors particular to the investors such as enterprise profitability and tax considerations.

Project development finance was evolving. Newer, more flexible approaches allowed fund providers to consider a company's cash flows and earnings as the source of funds that could repay an investment (or a loan). I learned the latter approach firsthand while opening new branches for Citibank in Central America, just as ADELA was breaking into that market. A half-century later the *Economist* echoed commonplace financial wisdom: "everyone agrees that ...cash flow matters most when valuing a firm or trying to work out if it might go bust." But in 1964, ADELA had not yet adopted that rule of corporate finance.

Saltex, a cement block producer in San Salvador, approached Citibank and ADELA for financing. ADELA insisted that any loan be supported by the principals' personal guarantees as well as the right to buy a minority equity position. Citibank El Salvador asked for a five-year cash-flow projection to support the loan request. Amusingly, President Lou Chiurato responded: "So what's a cash flow we ask, is it a loan without guarantees?" Citibank granted the loan.

The Saltex case and other learning experiences in financing entrepreneurs, with Citibank, ADELA, and the Bulgarian-American Enterprise Fund, led me to develop something of a corollary to the cash flow approach: A nurturing relationship is essential to dealing with small- and medium-sized enterprises. It is better achieved if the investor is a lender and holds collateral than if the investor is a minority investor and has neither leverage nor influence through shareholding. Nurturing (some call it mothering) is at the heart of developing small, newer businesses. Holding collateral, usually the borrower's productive facilities, provides the leverage for the lender to step in opportunely to guide borrowers and help when they get into trouble. The process is never smooth and requires a minimum legal backing for contracts and property rights. But it works.

The Saltex case is instructive. Citibank's money financed the purchase of a dredge for extracting sand from a river bed. Before long the dredge got stuck, production was delayed, and the loan was in trouble. The dredge became known as "Citibank's machine." I was in trouble with people in our New York head office who had feared from the beginning that the loan was too risky. Nevertheless, we facilitated getting technical assistance, restructured the loan, and nervously waited for better news. It came, and the dredge was put back in service. Lou's message to me: "When ADELA chickened out I was left holding the bag. We were known as the best bad debt of Citibank, but paid up." Today, Saltex is possibly Central America's best cement block producer.

Another practical example was set by the Latin American Agricultural Development Corporation (LAAD), a private firm owned by a dozen U.S. companies including Caterpillar, John Deere, Bank of America, and ADELA. LAAD's mission paralleled ADELA's: to promote agribusiness investment in rural Latin America. Incidentally, two former ADELA people managed LAAD, Tom Mooney and Bob Ross; and many of LAAD's shareholders were also shareholders of ADELA.

LAAD's equity investments had not been particularly successful. As it saw little prospect for sales of equity holdings that would permit it to avoid the risk of illiquidity, LAAD early switched to lending. Many of its best clients had to be rescheduled at least once during its first decade of operations, and again during the second decade. But, as its principals stated: "If LAAD had abandoned all of its projects which were in serious trouble, it would have lost most of its best clients. It would also probably have failed." Instead, LAAD continues lending to Latin American agribusiness to this day, usefully and profitably.

The U.S.-sponsored Enterprise Funds have practiced development financing using a mix of equity and loans pragmatically, as ADELA learned to do late in its saga. I have mentioned one in particular above, the Bulgarian-American Enterprise Fund (BAEF), where I was a director for nineteen years. The BAEF, which is fairly typical of the other Enterprise Funds, worked out a strategy for adapting its investment mandate to the vagaries of newly independent Bulgaria by investing in local vehicles that fund the entrepreneur through means other than straight equity investments. One was a leasing company that bought and owned property and equipment that it rented to entrepreneurs who might not yet qualify for the standard commercial bank loan. The other vehicle was a bank that, in the words of its CEO, did "secured lending to grey risks" among small and medium-sized businesses. The bank's deal-oriented lending officers structured loan repayments to fit expected cash flows, and in return collected equity-type fees for the bank. The managers of a government-owned hotel on the Black Sea that was being privatized would seek financing to purchase and renovate the hotel. Using the hotel as collateral, they could obtain a five-year loan from the bank with repayments scheduled just in the months matching the tourist flow from

May to September. The bank, which was then completely owned and operated by the BAEF, did more than 150 such loans. In fact, the bank pioneered term lending and became the predominant lender to all kinds of SMEs (small and medium-sized enterprises) across the country. The bank went on to be rated "The Best Bank in Bulgaria" among thirty-five banks, most of which, like Citibank, were subsidiaries of large foreign financial institutions.

ADELA was slow to try straight lending. Its annual reports repeatedly announced that it was in business to make "capital investments." Equity investing made sense in some instances, such as in the new pulp and paper project in Brazil, but in the same year as the paper project, ADELA invested $1 million in a family-owned textile mill in Honduras and found itself locked in for the next eighteen years. There was no stock exchange. The other outside funding sources, the IFC and government-owned development institutions, were lenders not shareholders; and ADELA was frozen out of governance and into passive, uncompensated shareholding. What worked in one environment, like big, industrial São Paulo, Brazil, didn't necessarily work in another, like small, rural Tegucigalpa, Honduras.

In the early days, ADELA made loans to investee companies that needed more financing. Under Ernst Keller, ADELA's first president, who served from its founding in September 1964 until he resigned in October 1975, the company had little disposition to try non-equity-related financing as a strategic alternative. A Swiss national, Keller had a dozen years of industrial financing experience in Peru with the W.R. Grace organization. He was also an entrepreneur who established at least two of his own companies in Peru.

Keller faced shareholder reluctance to let ADELA operate in activities similar to theirs (for the bank shareholders of ADELA, it was lending). Eventually, of course, ADELA got into lending. Although the price of learning was steep, as in Jamaica, the later Mexican, Chilean, and Colombian operations, among others, were professionally and profitably conducted.

ADELA failed to recognize consciously that it had become involved in two different businesses and to discern how to structure itself to do both. One of its businesses was matching funding and partners for large equity deals in more-developed markets. The other was funding small entrepreneurs in undeveloped financial markets, which required the approach of a small country banker.

5. The People of ADELA and How They Operated

⌒

The air was heady with deals and doings at headquarters in Lima, Peru, during ADELA's early years. A high point was the annual staff meeting, usually held at the Lima Country Club, when Peter Drucker, the father of modern management, joined his friend Ernst Keller. Drucker had come to know Keller through his earlier association with W.R. Grace and Co., which had its nineteenth century origins in Peru, and which was run (for forty-eight years) by Drucker's friend Peter Grace. As a managing director described it:

> Drucker would come to Lima and listen to the wonderful stories being told, and then pontificate. It was all quite fascinating to be in the presence of this management guru, and we soaked up every word. It was all pretty heady, and we basked in his praise. Drucker believed that the ADELA team was an extraordinary bunch of young wizards doing marvelous things. If he knew of and/or suspected the problems, he was careful to avoid mentioning them. He and Keller had their own mutual admiration society and it was interesting to sit back and watch them eulogize each other. Drucker was fascinated by the fact that EK had assembled a coalition of the largest MNCs (multinational companies) in the free world, and was doing venture capital in Latin America.

The reality was otherwise. ADELA's early successes were achieved on the abilities of CEO Keller and a very few good men. But continued expansion required a trained cadre of investment managers and a much more formal system of risk management. ADELA needed managers skilled in risk analysis, knowledgeable about the places they would invest in, and supported by an independent capability for vetting projects.

As ADELA grew, and it grew rapidly in the first five years, it "hired green business school graduates to spread its funds among hundreds of ventures," wrote John Train. It may not have been hyperbole for the *Wall Street Journal* to state that "young men fresh out of Harvard and Stanford business schools were making the key decisions." One manager reminisced to me about "the tremendous gap between developing country conditions and professionals trained to develop business opportunities in more sophisticated environments, like me coming from Wall Street with nothing but an MBA and three years of private placement experience (which I never used at ADELA). And it was not easy to bring someone from Switzerland into Quito in the 60s and find that he had much to offer from his experience."

Another staffer criticized bringing in foreign managers who were unfamiliar with the place and the ways of doing business. "Seldom," he wrote, "does this bring success; you have to use the local people to manage. In Brazil, ADELA had a team of ten to twelve professionals—all gringos (foreigners) —not one single Brazilian in management until the late 1970s. This I think was one of the flaws in the foundations of ADELA." By contrast, in Mexico, after the management team became local, the results turned quite positive.

But ADELA's high turnover made it certain that green graduates would continue to fill the posts of the investment analysts. One staffer, who became something of a whistle-blower, wrote to a managing director: "Frankly the turnover rate of ADELA officers and professional staff is appalling. By actual count in January of 1969 the company had hired two people for each one retained. The standard greeting at regional meetings: 'Are you still with us?' is really a sharp-edged statement."

The problem was not only with green graduates who were getting their training on-the-job, but also with ADELA's unmanaged expansion. By its fifth year ADELA had invested some $200 million in 102 projects (roughly $1.4 billion in today's dollars). And in that year, the company added to the burden of watching over so many investments by creating a Venture Capital Fund for small enterprises. In the following twelve months the fund invested $1.3 million in 27 projects of small enterprises, with each investment averaging less than $50,000 each. At its height, ADELA had four-hundred loans and investments being managed by a staff of only sixty, at least half of whom were not out in the field offices. A senior manager wrote to me

> One BIG mistake of policy...was allowing such a large number of small investments in all conceivable fields of activity scattered throughout the continent. I think this made it very difficult, if not impossible, for management to properly manage the investment portfolio. This led to many failures and losses.

How could so few managers have presumed to nurture all those investments? John Train's answer was that they simply could not. In 1972, as ADELA was increasing its income by 35 percent to $6.6 million and preparing to trumpet its accomplishments in a brochure, Train was writing to fellow director, Bert Witham, then vice-president of finance at IBM:

> I find that within the operating management and among directors and others who have regular contact with the company at the operating level, particularly with the regional offices, there is a feeling that while the purposes of ADELA are fine, the execution is not competent. (That is not strange. It is, after all, very hard to make money.) ADELA does seem to me to function

more like an industry association or even a government bureau than like a profit-making company. One place this really shows up is in the people. In the ADELA structure I have met barely a handful I consider truly able, seasoned business men, who know how to make money with money. (There are many—probably too many—inexperienced although intelligent and energetic young men who can turn out studies. Unfortunately this is not a young man's game, nor a graduate school.) The turnover is remarkable, and one often hears when someone goes that basically he was not very capable.

Inevitably, ADELA courted trouble when its reach exceeded the CEO's grasp. A chasm loomed between the field officers' lack of experience and the level of professionalism required. Said Tom Mooney, ADELA's manager for Central America: "When I joined ADELA I knew the territory, knew how business was done there and who was doing it. The ADELA managers of the other territories came in as strangers and this hurt them and ADELA (more so)." This was highly evident in Jamaica, which may not have represented a microcosm of ADELA, but it illustrated much that was troubling about ADELA's first decade, even as the company was recording impressive results.

The Jamaica Experience

As the salesman said in *The Music Man,* "He doesn't know the territory." ADELA failed to get that message. In 1972 it sent to Jamaica a European chargé who was new to the place and to the business. According to an official, CEO Keller hired the chargé as a sort of secretary in Europe and then brought him over as such to company headquarters in Lima, Peru. He wrote to a friend: "I was recommended to Ernst Keller in 1970 by the management of Lampe Bank, a shareholder of ADELA.

They even paid for my first class return ticket to Zurich where I first met Ernst who subsequently hired me...I came to Lima in April—I believe—of 1971."

Real estate salesmen were calling alluringly, but underneath rang warning tones that high taxes and fears of communism were driving out the middle class, who would be the buyers for ADELA-financed urbanized lots and apartments. "Out" meant out of Jamaica. During the 1970s, eight years of badl government were devastating Jamaica; unfortunately, the country was being brought to economic collapse by spending more than it earned on a range of social and economic programs. If one didn't know the country and what was happening, and didn't know the real estate business, one couldn't possibly figure out how to structure a project to mitigate the risks—if indeed such a way could have been found.

In less than two years, between 1973 and 1975, ADELA made twelve separate three-year loans totaling $14 million to finance real estate development. Almost from the start the projects were burdened with problems such as cost overruns, poor sales, and hitches in hooking up to basic services, all of which translated into difficulties servicing the loans. The borrowing companies were little more than vehicles contrived on the spur of the moment to obtain ADELA's financing. One ADELA analyst explained: "Everybody loved ADELA and welcomed ADELA for its money—not necessarily its expertise." An additional and eventually insurmountable hurdle was that the loans were in dollars while project sales were in local currency, which steadily depreciated against the dollar. By the time I joined ADELA five years later in 1978, all but one of the borrowers were defunct, and all of the loans were nonperforming.

Why make a million-dollar loan every six weeks or so for developing pieces of land without pausing early on to evaluate the situation? Why even make the first loan without knowing the business, the borrower, and the environment? Why, for that matter, did ADELA need to be in Jamaica at all during those years? I haven't found answers other than to observe that ADELA, propelled by substantial available funding, was on a big expansion kick. Apparently that explains why it also made two isolated investments on the island of Trinidad, which failed as well. ADELA seemed to want to be everywhere in the Americas.

The due diligence for the Jamaican loans, the process through which lenders investigate and evaluate borrowers, was done in Kingston, where the first loans may have seemed particularly appealing when the minister of finance, who was en route to becoming prime minister, recommended them. To be fair, pressure locally and from Lima to make loans must have weighed heavily on ADELA's representative in Jamaica. The new board of management, comprising four regional senior managing directors, each zealously guarding their turf, was to review and approve the Jamaica loans in Lima, Peru. Rafael Morales, who became executive vice president in my regime in 1968, and who had a degree in engineering from Massachusetts Institute of Technology, ten years in consulting and construction activities for several major oil companies, plus experience as a director of the Colombian National Development Bank, described the situation to me like this:

> I clearly remember Gene Gonzalez, who would become president for a year, following CEO Keller's withdrawal in 1975, commenting to me after some of the meetings of the Board of Management that ADELA's man in Jamaica was the star of the field officers because he was number one in amounts disbursed and in earned fees...The famous fees simply came from the loans themselves. The borrowers never disbursed a single penny out of their pockets. Yet the fees were automatically booked as income in ADELA. To my knowledge, the four man board in Lima was not supported by anyone knowledgeable about the real estate business in Jamaica or anywhere else.

Compare this with the system used, for example, by the smaller Bulgarian-American Enterprise Fund. The BAEF, doing venture investing in post-communist Bulgaria, devised its real estate lending policies and procedures from systems that U.S. banks used for many years. The system works like this: when a potential borrower requests a loan, a real estate group independent of the lending officers reviews the project and the construction budget and tests the reasonableness of the assumptions. In addition, the real estate group determines whether the project meets predetermined parameters:

- At least 25 percent of the total Project budget has to be invested by the borrower before loan funds are disbursed.
- The value of collateral available in the project (the property being developed, plus whatever the promoters own in the way of apartments, stores, offices, or garages) must be at least 133 percent of the total loan amount for residential projects.
- The construction budget under the loan must include *all* costs necessary to complete the project.
- Once the loan is approved by the credit committee, disbursements are made corresponding to the discrete phases of the construction program—with each subsequent disbursement authorized only after review on site and against budget.
- Disbursement of the final tranche is contingent upon a review of any permits still to be obtained.

At last review, the BAEF's construction program totaled 105 loans, with only one default in five years. That particular case involved a commitment to lend €2.7 million (US$3.2 million) to construct an apartment building. When troubles appeared after almost 1 million euros had been disbursed, the BAEF froze disbursements and took steps to take over the program and finish the project itself.

The IFC would later judge ADELA's real estate portfolio in Jamaica to be symptomatic of "an inadequate authority system, poor quality staff work, the absence of cross checks of project costs, and the inexistence of a system of review of loans and investments." Evidently ADELA Jamaica failed to heed reggae artist and activist Bob Marley's warning: "Don't let them fool you," for ADELA relied on sponsors' estimates, without outside checks, and without control procedures to see that borrowers used the funds for the stated purpose. Thus, ADELA wound up making additional loans to more than half its Jamaican loan portfolio, rather than call the loans and cut its costs. For example, the "Anchor" loan, made in 1973 for $700,000 to construct houses, was restructured the following year and then received three additional loans in 1975-6 for $110,000 each. A decade later, it was still on the books and in litigation, according to IFC's reports in 1979 after its review. The following year, when ADELA met with its creditors, they concluded:

> A workout plan for Jamaica is not feasible now; nobody is going to try to do anything there....No one is going to put his money in property and allied things in Jamaica now. It is not what can be done. There is stagnation, inflation and devaluation in Jamaica. Even if you sell something, you cannot get your money out of Jamaica because it is not convertible.

Recovery of the Jamaican portfolio proved daunting. ADELA Jamaica, in mid-1983, having failed IMF (International Monetary Fund) tests, moved remittances to the parallel market (read black market), thus provoking a de facto devaluation of more than 50 percent. By that time, only one of ADELA's ten remaining loans in Jamaica had been paid back; two were reactivated; three saw their underlying property sold; and four had yet to show possibilities of resolution. According to ADELA's senior management, the Jamaican operation cost ADELA some $20 million in direct loans and lost interest plus an indeterminate amount in wasted operating expenses—not only the ADELA representative's salary and fringes but also costs such as office expenses, travel, relocation, and support staff. This does not even include the millions of dollars of interest ADELA paid to the banks that had funded the Jamaica portfolio and costs accrued for time and frequent travel of ADELA senior officials who tried to recover these investments.

In the early years when transaction volume was still small, Keller could hop from office to office to show the field officers how to do their deals and check on the ones in progress. But even then, problems were building because this astute, confident leader failed to encourage initiatives to cut losses early. In 1970, one staffer wrote to a senior managing director: "I am distressed at the widespread feeling that the company takes its profits and lets losses run, and someday we will have to pay up." Peruvian boat-building, one of ADELA's earliest and largest investments made during Keller's peak years, was still claiming ADELA money and effort more than a decade later. The doomed project was not unique; others included floor-tile manufacturing in Brazil, rice-growing in Belize, and a host of others that consumed lots of money and executive time. It is instructive to look closer at three.

Building anchovy boats in Peru

The involvement with boat builder Metal Empresa started early in AD-ELA's saga. In 1965 ADELA approved a $1,200,000 loan to Promecon, reputedly among Peru's larger industrial enterprises. "Reputedly" because one ADELA staffer called it a bit of a stretch to invest hard dollars in a purely service company (i.e., "a bunch of engineers") with no assets to support the investment. The deal included an option to convert $600,000 of the loan into 20 percent of the company. Promecon was a creation of EK Associates (read Ernst Keller), and was one of ADELA's first involvements. Even as ADELA's very first annual report acknowledged difficulties with this investment, the company increased its exposure to $2 million through an additional loan of $800,000.

After ADELA joined Promecon's board, it became apparent that the company had real financial problems. At that point, ADELATEC (ADELA's technical consulting arm) was brought in under an eighteen-month contract to "perform management functions." ADELA then merged Promecon into Metal Empresa, a fishing, fishmeal, and ship-building complex (located thirty kilometers inland from the sea) that ADELA was just acquiring for $3,000,000. At first, it looked as if ADELA could provide the company with the technical and financial help it needed, and simultaneously arrange to eventually exit from the investment by bringing in a major Japanese ship builder that was also an ADELA shareholder. But disagreements with ADELA's president caused the Japanese to withdraw. For fifteen years ADELA's executives muddled along, putting more and more money into Metal Empresa, trying all kinds of initiatives but remaining stuck in a money-losing business.

Then along came a crisis in fishing, which had been Peru's key industry from the late 1950s to mid-'70s, when fleets of *bolicheros* (Creole for *small business*) plied the Pacific coast. The cause was El Niño (the little child), the warm current that arrives every so often around Christmas in the waters off Peru's coast and litters them with dead fish. In the late '70s it wrecked the fishing industry on the Pacific coast of Latin America. Metal Empresa suddenly lost its most important internal market, that of fishing vessels, and was unable to service its large foreign exchange debt. Its operating performance kept worsening, and in late 1980 ADELA had to restructure the company and capitalize loans amounting to US$900,000. By that time, ADELA had invested almost $8 million in Metal Empresa. According to a senior managing director, "this single example resulted in close to $25 million of losses if you add in the collateral and/or related damage it caused. A case study of Promecon would highlight all of the foibles and mistakes that led to ADELA's undoing." A few years later the company was sold to a brother-in-law of an ADELA senior staffer, thus relieving ADELA of potential labor obligations, but for a token price.

Tile manufacturing in Brazil

Martini was an old (1912) family business that produced clay sewer pipes. In 1969, after ADELA opened a São Paulo office and accumulated almost a dozen expatriate staffers, it paid $550,000 for a 36 percent interest in Martini. The investment was to bolster Martini's capital for expanding sewer pipe production and adding production of ceramic tiles for kitchen and bath. After the initial funding, Martini asked ADELA for more money but never invited them to sit in on family councils where plans were formulated and intramural disputes aired. Business custom or the legal system did not yet guarantee the foreign minority voice a hearing.

ADELA's exclusion was unfortunate because Martini's cash-eating expansion was proving, to say the least, overly ambitious and unguided. The required financing simply wasn't available, and technical problems surfaced. When the first OPEC oil embargo in 1974 caused fuel prices to climb, the market crumbled, and Martini was saddled with heavy debt. Moreover, family members were disputing management succession from the patriarch to a headstrong scion. Meanwhile, ADELA was unable to provide the wise and steadying influence that its cachet implied. Three years earlier, it had created ADELATEC to provide professional support to develop investments into viable projects. But that expertise could not prevent Martini from over-expanding and taking on too much debt.

Ultimately the investment in Martini proved to be very unsuccessful. ADELA never received interest on its loans or dividends on its equity. Finally, in the late 1980s, Martini went bankrupt. The liquidation favored the workers, tax authorities (Martini owed $17 million in taxes and social security payments), and Brazilian banks. ADELA lost its entire $5 million investment.

Rice growing in Belize

ADELA's fifth annual report first mentioned Big Falls Rice Ranch as a new investment. It consisted of a $500,000 capital subscription plus a loan of $37,000 in a start-up operation. In actuality, according to a later report by the IFC, Big Falls had been historically unprofitable. It was located in Belize (which did not change its name from British Honduras until 1973), about which Aldous Huxley wrote: "If the world had any ends, British Honduras would certainly be one of them. It is not on the way from anywhere to anywhere else. It has no strategic value. It is all but uninhabited." Tom Mooney, ADELA's man in charge of Central America, turned down the proposal to invest in Big Falls: "It was an obvious loser and would have been laughable if ADELA had elected to finance it. Much to my surprise it did, in spite of my opinion of it." After Tom left ADELA, his successor, a recently graduated MBA, became anxious to proceed with the project. Tom wrote to me: "I didn't know for several months after I left ADELA that the financial participation in Big Falls had been approved by ADELA in Lima (headquarters). That, I thought, was inconceivable. It would have been no less logical to undertake the project in the Darien Gap (a large swath of underdeveloped swamp land separating Panama and Colombia) with no management or knowledge." The investment in Big Falls, as it turned out, was ADELA's worst loss.

In the ADELA report of 1970, a new American shareholder appeared—Kern County Land Company (subsequently changed to Tenneco, which purchased Kern County), with shares valued, it appears, for the amount of the investment in the rice farm. How opportune for Tenneco to rid itself of a sticky involvement in a backwater place and gain in return a membership in a do-good club of peers offering a window on a part of the world that could become a market for the tractors and farm implements it manufactured. For ADELA too it could have seemed a bargain to acquire majority interest in a 33,000-acre farm in exchange for paper shares of ADELA, which cost it nothing, and a $37,000 loan to the American family that owned a minority stockholding and operated the farm. If they couldn't pay, ADELA could take the farm, and so it did. Ten years and $9 million later, ADELA had long since foreclosed on the farm and was still trying to make it viable. Finally, in the 1980s, ADELA gave up and ceded the place to the Belize government.

Unfortunately, the land at Big Falls was suboptimal for growing rice. Besides poor soil, which takes years to improve, high tropical temperatures are less than felicitous for growing rice. Failing to recognize soil and climate factors, ADELA kept investing a lot of money in a losing battle against Mother Nature. Of course, they brought in world-wide experts and consultants for advice, but they could not change the fundamental problems. Rafael Morales, who liquidated ADELA's remaining investments, including Big Falls Rice Farm, remembered that rice cultivation on Big Falls yielded at most about 3,000 pounds per acre, four or five times smaller than yields in rice-growing regions of the United States, Surinam, South America, and the Far East. Obviously, the project had not the slightest chance of being competitive or successful.

These three disparate ADELA investments—one a going concern in its home port at the outset of its voyage, another in a factory expansion in Latin America's largest and most industrialized city, and a third in agriculture occurring at midcourse far away in a tiny British protectorate—are not necessarily representative of the five-hundred projects ADELA initiated in its first decade in so many activities, situations, and places. Yet, the three experiences offer practical examples of why the ADELA venture investment model, and the way it was applied, was unworkable. We can tick off the reasons

- Capital was tied up unproductively for years. ADELA received no income to contribute to overhead.
- No formal, effective avenue existed for exiting the investments. ADELA was trapped, whatever crisis might arise.
- Being both investor and lender in the same company put ADELA in conflict with itself. A shareholder explained: "It isn't easy to call a loan when you also have equity in the same firm. If you call the loan you risk dumping the company into bankruptcy. And that could cost you your original investment."
- Veteran investors who could provide guidance, or know where to get it, were unavailable. ADELA was technically incompetent in consulting, even with ADELATEC, which never built up the ethos and systems of a McKinsey, yet nevertheless embarked on numerous consulting and development projects. The reality of venture capitalism, as has been said ad infinitum, is that it is partly a matter of selecting and vetting the right investments, and even more of managing and nurturing firms. That means having savvy investment managers able to spend time with each investee—a practice that limits the number of commitments investors can take on.
- Minority shareholdings have no real voice in decision making. Martini was the norm in this regard, not the exception.

ADELA's chief executive, Ernst Keller, failed to see the need to take such factors into account. In an interview with *Forbes* in 1974, he remarked: "...since we'll never make a killing on any of our investments, we must bring home virtually all of them." Yet three of the biggest—tile production, rice growing, and anchovy-ship building—never came home. Those cases were not unique. Consider Studio 501, a furniture maker right in ADELA's front yard, Lima,

Peru. ADELA purchased a minority share in 1969 for $900,000. By 1981, when our new management set about to rehabilitate the firm, ADELA's exposure had risen to almost $4 million in an asset that had produced zero earnings for ADELA in twelve years.

On leaving ADELA, I went through the files and culled the largest twenty-five investments (including the four mentioned above) that ADELA had made in its first decade and that were still nonperforming as its second decade was ending. The total exposure was an astounding $88 million. Most of this outlay had not been carried by capital but by borrowed money on which interest was being paid year in and year out.

Here, growth was the enemy of investment quality. The CEO was no longer able to review all loans and investments and was forced to pass authority to approve deals to inexperienced managers in field offices. The CEO needed, instead, a formal risk-analysis training program backed by a system of policies and procedures for managing risk that would have included *functioning* credit and investment committees at regional or country office levels. The board, for its part, needed to back this up with checks and balances provided by a strong internal audit group along with audit and investment committees. An investment company, like any business, must have internal auditors—independent and skeptical—to check that deals are conducted properly and reported in accordance with company policy and procedure. A board must have directors' committees to monitor and liaison with the audit group and the credit committee, which is how boards get the real work of governance done. ADELA's expansion was accomplished without such controls, and without a cadre of experienced senior managers to guide and support the junior ones. Yet the Board of Directors hardly demurred.

About ADELA's management

I ultimately blame ADELA's board for failing in its fiduciary responsibility to oversee management and make necessary course corrections. Although certainly enough blame can be cast about, what is the responsibility of oversight if not to act when management goes wrong?

Don Nicholson was a graduate of University of Pennsylvania's Wharton School of Finance, and his first employment was with Fidelity Bank of Philadelphia. After a short apprenticeship, Howard Peterson, the bank's chairman, seconded Don to ADELA where Peterson was then vice chairman. Don opened the Brazil office for ADELA and built its loans and investments to $100 million. He sees "a different cast of characters as the real perpetrators of the debacle." From his perspective, "the real villain was management, with me [himself] included."

In discussing the Jamaican portfolio above, I mentioned the IFC's critique as symptomatic of unsound risk-management practices company-wide. Later I shall explain why the IFC was called in to look at decision-making in ADELA and the consequences of that invitation. But first we can look at the evolution of ADELA's management organization and practices in the Keller era and its aftermath.

In 1970, ADELA's fifth year, Keller elected to decentralize management. Undoubtedly, he found he wasn't indefatigable: there were simply too many projects and offices to visit as was his custom. (An additional reason has been suggested: President Velasco Alvarado had taken over the Peruvian government, making it impossible to continue running ADELA from Peru.)

So, Keller assigned managing directors, each responsible for a geographic territory, each with authority to approve loans and investments. Those five directors, with Keller, constituted a board of management to review and approve larger transactions. In setting up this board, Keller seems to have been preparing for succession. He made two of them senior managing directors and then anointed one, Harry Reuss, as his heir. However, Reuss left the company when he fell out of favor for his handling of the Capsa affair. Starting in 1966, ADELA invested more than $7 million in Capsa, a Paraguayan company that processed cooking oil, cotton fiber, and tobacco. Capsa got into trouble, and ADELA was forced to take over its management to protect the company's large investment. The other senior managing director, Gene Gonzalez, who succeeded Keller, commented later that the board of management never worked well because Keller put the four in "acute competition" with each other.

This was not a "team of rivals," in the Lincoln cabinet mold, nor was it a group of constructively competitive potential successors as practiced by Walter Wriston at Citibank. The four members of ADELA's board of management openly resisted each other. Their areas became fiefdoms, zealously guarded. Moreover, now that each "lord" had authority to approve his own loans and investments, each did so right up to the limit of that authority—and defended his turf against the other lords. Pete Collado, who stepped from ADELA's board into the presidency when Gonzalez resigned, told about visiting one region and eavesdropping on a meeting at the home of a senior managing director. He heard the fellow admonishing the troops not to tell the big boss from New York anything, just refer all questions to him.

By 1975, when Keller decided to leave, "for health reasons," he may well have become disenchanted by what a senior official at the IFC described as the "inordinate amount of time the four managing directors spent in Machiavellian back stabbing." Indeed, more than one ADELA insider opined that Keller saw the problems building and, to escape blame, left before the ship sank. Argentine diplomat Alejandro Orfila, who established ADELA's rep office in Washington, DC, for Keller and channeled some projects to the company, was close to ADELA's inner workings. He told me that Keller had surrounded himself with weak people who were simply not business managers. Incidentally, one project that Orfila steered to ADELA, Agrodinámica (cattle raising and meat processing) in Central America, profited him handsomely when it was sold. Orfila later served as secretary general of the Organization of American States between 1975 and 1984.

Gene Gonzalez had come from the bureaucracy of the Inter-American Development Bank. The arrangement proved unworkable and lasted barely a year. One ADELA staffer wrote to me that the decision was a disaster: "Even weak leadership is preferable to divided leadership." The team of peers had become a team of paranoids. In selecting the senior man as president, ADELA's board seemed to have taken the easy way out. It seems inconceivable that the board did not know that Gonzalez had not demonstrated managerial qualities. The way succession was handled after Keller left would become an important factor in ADELA's collapse.

"Internal squabbling led to inaction in the face of problems. The poisoned climate made the best executives look for other jobs, and the company began to unravel," said one managing director. Indeed, greatly because of the resignations, ADELA's condition deteriorated noticeably. It took a year before the directors noted that few mature senior managers were still around. Pete Collado, a founding director, then stepped out of retirement from Esso, where he had been an executive vice president, and agreed to serve as president of ADELA. He served from late 1976 until October 1979, when he yielded to me at the board meeting in Stockholm. I, along with a crew assembled mainly from ADELA veteran professionals, assumed the responsibility for carrying out Pete's reorganization of ADELA. Just before we began, the Sandinistas overthrew Somoza in Nicaragua, and a civil war began that would devastate the country. What an omen for the task before us.

It may be forgotten how bad things had become in Latin America as the 1980s began. The one exemplary economy, the free market represented by Chile, had "utterly collapsed by the early '80s," in the words of an MIT professor. Nearly every bank in Chile went under, including a bank that ADELA had invested in.

As an aside, walking down a New York City street early that year, I ran into George Moore, retired Citibank chairman, and told him that I had recently left my job as CEO for INCO's nickel project in Guatemala, just after production had begun, to join ADELA. His reaction startled me: "You fool, didn't you look into it first?" In his staccato style, he snapped through ADELA's problems: failed management, bad investments, shareholders who no longer cared, Latin America in trouble. Nevertheless, from this chance encounter, we began a series of meetings at River House whenever he returned to New York from retirement in Spain. During those meetings I filled him in on happenings at ADELA. He gave me good advice, and occasionally he went to bat for us with our bankers. But ADELA's situation had become intractable, as you will see.

In early 1978, Stanley Penn reported in the *Wall Street Journal* ("Faded Dream") that some of ADELA's backers had begun to have second thoughts about its achievements and way of doing business. Among the concerns: controversial accounting methods that painted a rosier picture than was justified; a lawsuit in New York Federal Court brought by two of ADELA's partners about its ethics in promoting a loan to a Mexican client; investments that were faring poorly—as evidenced by the fact that almost two-thirds of the company investees were not profitable; some of the biggest investments that were known to be in trouble; the company throwing good money after bad into many investments; and too much responsibility being placed on the shoulders of its tiny management staff. Penn's article could have been a belated wake-up call to the governors and directors. But ADELA's leaders responded by circling the wagons. In letters to the editor and elsewhere, Senator Javits, former CEO Keller, and current President Collado, all shot back in fierce de-

71

fense. They claimed that Penn showed a "frightful ignorance about the nature of ADELA's business" and didn't get a true picture of ADELA because his sources of information were, as Keller stated, "former ADELA employees who took great pains to remain anonymous, [which was] quite understandable in view of their performance in ADELA."

Yet signs as well as allegations of trouble had been appearing for almost a decade before the Penn article. In 1970, an ADELA manager wrote to a member of the Board of Management citing, in addition to low salaries, two recurrent themes among people within the company: a belief that the company was in trouble financially, and dismay at the company's approach toward profit realization. After I joined ADELA, he sent me a copy. Among specific charges were these:

- "The company takes its profits and lets losses run, and someday we will have to pay up.
- The company is improperly booking profits, taking into current income much that should be deferred over the periods of the operation.
- The company appears to be carrying large amounts of accounts receivable, which are in fact probably not recoverable.
- The company should not be booking share dividends as profits.
- The reserves [for losses] have been chiefly used in order to show net profit growth."

In 1974, *Forbes Magazine* reported that a good number of ADELA-backed new ventures had run into serious difficulties. About that time, ADELA's external auditors disagreed with management about reserves for losses. The auditors were subsequently replaced. Actually, throughout the decade of the '70s, various sources, including some of ADELA's owners, voiced concerns about the way

ADELA operated and the condition of its investment portfolio.

How ADELA's managers funded its growth

ADELA's game plan, from the beginning, was aggressive expansion. The company made forty-four investments in its first year, and in its fourth and fifth years it disbursed $300 million in loans and investments. The top three executives, CEO Keller, EVP Gonzalez, and EVP Reuss (the CAPSA reorganizer) were "promoting and selling ADELA to everyone," according to one ADELA senior managing director.

The problem with ADELA's fast growth was not just how to manage it but how to fund it. ADELA quickly tied up its capital in long-term investments, of which two-thirds, as reporter Penn noted, came to consist of unprofitable companies. As funds generated from profits were insufficient to cover investment needs, ADELA funded its continued expansion with money borrowed from banks that were flush with petro-dollars. In the 1970s, major oil-producing states earned more money from the export of oil than they could usefully invest in their own economies. They deposited their huge surpluses of petro-dollars in U.S. and European commercial banks. Recession in the developed economies prompted those banks to look to developing countries, especially in Central and South America, as places to lend this money. That proved to be terribly expensive to the borrowers.

ADELA borrowed first from its shareholder banks. Then it widened the circle to include banks outside the ADELA family. In fact, said a managing director, when Gonzalez's turn at the top came, "he didn't care where the funds were borrowed, just about having the tombstones of the deals published." (Tombstones are written advertisements that investment bankers place to boast a public offering of a security.) In the crucial five years before Keller departed, the company's borrowings more than doubled, from $154 million to $341 million, to finance its lending and investing activities, which had grown to more than $400 million ($1.9 billion in today's dollars). The company's own capital funds supporting this expansion grew at less than half the rate of borrowings. By the time our new management team took over in 1979, the company's debt-to-equity ratio had reached 5.3:1. It was relying five times more on borrowing than on capital to fund its business.

ADELA borrowed where and how it could, and this meant sometimes having to borrow short term to fund investments that would pay off only over a longer term. This behavior foreshadowed the 2007 U.S. real estate financing bubble, in which, among other things, long-term assets—real estate—were financed by hedge funds using short-term debt. In ADELA's case, a maturity imbalance was created in which ADELA would have to pay back loans before its portfolio produced the wherewithal. A large part of the loans would be owed to non-shareholder banks.

Had ADELA borrowed only from shareholder banks, it could conceivably have restructured those loans and maybe even capitalized some of the debt, and thereby might have had a chance to survive, as some in management and on its board suggested. But ADELA failed to restrict itself to in-house borrowing, although it was against policy to borrow outside. In corroboration, ADELA Chairman Bert Witham (IBM's treasurer) wrote Keller:

> A really big mistake, in my opinion, was the fact that we departed from what I thought was an understood principle that when it comes to borrowing we would only borrow from our shareholders. The fact that we ended up borrowing from IFC, which has been the most troublesome of all of our creditors, plus a lot of others that were involved in the syndicate, such as the Singer Friedlander syndicate, we had more than we could handle; whereas we could have recovered, and I think rather quickly,

had we had only our shareholders as creditors. I think we could have worked out an arrangement and an accommodation and brought ADELA back to good health in a relatively short time.

Here is how Keller replied: "I am not surprised that some of the finance houses prove difficult to deal with. I would not have thought ever of having them syndicate a loan for ADELA. I also advised Gene Gonzalez against taking ADELA to the public markets." Keller understood that ADELA's investments in developing companies could not return the necessary cash to fulfill commitments to pay back loans according to the rigid timetables of commercial banks. At any rate, when ADELA chose to borrow funds on the market, it marked the beginning of a new direction. Decisions on how to apply its funds would be controlled not only by its board and management, but also by its bankers, who would not have the same interest or long-term view as its shareholders. Rafael Morales believed that the biggest blunder was to involve non-shareholder financial institutions in ADELA's funding. Don Nicholson, ADELA's CFO under Pete Collado, seconded this:

> The initial concept was sound that is to borrow from shareholder banks in order to leverage ADELA's equity and thereby have added resources that would improve the overall ROI (return on investment). The strategy went astray when ADELA started making long out of short and using the lines (of credit) to refinance non-performing loans. Intermediate term loans were also a good idea in that it gave ADELA longer term leverage and the ability to run a matched loan book (i.e. the maturities of the funds borrowed by ADELA would be matched by the maturities of the funds it lent). Again it went astray by the conscious decision to keep pumping in added funding to situations such as Metal Empresa and Capsa that were incapable of repaying and/or servicing the loans.

A second way that ADELA financed its activities was by selling its loans in the New York market. This became more and more important for raising cash as ADELA found it increasingly difficult to borrow from banks. Moreover, other institutions were already placing Latin American paper on the New York market, like the very successful investment banking house of Leslie Weinert. This firm was led by Peter Leslie, a former Citibanker, who had trained in Brazil, and Richard Weinert, who specialized in international syndications. Accordingly, toward the mid-1970s, Keller formed ADELA Securities. I believe he intended to become a major player in placing Latin American private debt paper in the New York market by exploiting ADELA's on-the-spot familiarity with Latin American enterprises. ADELA Securities, located in New York City, was run by an astute veteran who knew the business, and it was profitable from the start. But after Keller's withdrawal it became mainly a vehicle for generating cash by selling off ADELA's loans. It was a major undertaking through which a substantial portion of ADELA's loan portfolio—"mostly the good stuff" said an ADELA senior—was divested. Some of the loans sold had to be repurchased when Latin American economic conditions deteriorated so drastically in the late '70s, which provoked criticism by some in ADELA and by members of the Review Committee (more about that later).

To give the reader a feel for the cost of ADELA's borrowings, I quote from a memo in January 1980 by Robert McNamara, then president of the World Bank and its subsidiary, the IFC. He reported to his board that "the large and growing volume of non-income producing loan and equity investments in ADELA's portfolio totaled $152 million; ...one-half of those non-income producing investments were being funded with Eurodollar borrowings that were costing ADELA over $1 million per month." (This was, I might add, because interest rates had more than doubled by 1981 to 16.5 percent, and then rose further to 18 percent.)

76

CEO Keller maintained that cautious management of borrowings and maintenance of high liquidity had been hallmarks of his stewardship, and that the principle was shelved after he retired. But Don Nicholson, ADELA's manager in Brazil and later CFO, thought: "the errors, misjudgments and omissions that occurred during EK's [Ernst Keller's] tenure doomed the company from the very beginning. Go back and review the situation just before EK left, when Harry Reuss was seen as the anointed successor. Every major problem was already in place, just waiting to happen." Keller must share the blame, with his management team, for being reluctant to admit mistakes, to cut losses early, and to portray the company's true condition accurately. The Board of Directors, for its part, failed to referee the company's borrowing program.

Yet some of the directors—those representing shareholder banks—tried zealously to keep ADELA out of their business (as, for example, other shareholders did about keeping ADELA from investing in oil) and became vociferously critical when it did. Now they saw ADELA as competition. Richard Boyle, a perceptive member of the Lima staff, wrote: "ADELA's very success in developing a quality portfolio of short and medium term Latin American loans had opened the eyes of its shareholder banks to the profits to be earned in this field."

Now, you don't have to be a bank to lend money. General Electric Commercial Finance was not a bank. Yet in 2006 its portfolio of commercial and industrial loans, at $230 billion, was more than the commercial and industrial portfolios of Bank of America and JP Morgan Chase combined. The BAEF investment group in Bulgaria, with no experience in banking, and just a few years as a lender, found it relatively straightforward to start a bank. When the BAEF started its bank, I was the only person in the group who had had any banking experience, and I had been out of banking for twenty-eight years. In the twelve years that followed, that bank regularly earned the highest marks from banking examiners, while consistently reporting high profits. An IPO in early

2006 for 30 percent of the bank attracted buyers from all over Europe who paid a premium of 4.7 times net book value—possibly a record. Said George Moore, when he was chairman of Citibank, "If you're not actually stupid or dishonest, it is hard not to make money in banking."

As a banker, ADELA was lending at medium term—three to five years. It got into the business by financing companies in which it held shares. Keller saw this lending function for what it was, as he wrote to the *Wall Street Journal:* "Much of its [ADELA's] loans are just another form of venture capital, ahead of and more secure than, equity investments."

The problem was that "venture capital" type loans were not producing the income to power ADELA's pursuit of growth and to pay the earnings-based bonuses that the senior field managers had become accustomed to. One senior managing director wrote to me that a "second activity, banking, took on a life of its own. It wasn't development work, but a way to create income." Lending wasn't a bad idea, or an activity that they couldn't master, even if the banker shareholders could not agree. LAAD, also operating in Latin America, became a successful lender and remains so today. But lending must be done right.

The key to successful lending is a risk-management system based on well-defined policies and procedures. The name of the lending game is financial risk management. The problem at ADELA was that it had failed to develop an appropriate lending system. Luis Valenzuela, an ADELA vice president in its Mexico City office, saw that clearly.

Luis was a Mexican national with a degree in business administration from Arizona State University and graduate work at the prestigious Instituto Panamericana de Alta Dirección de Empresa of Mexico. He spent three years with Citibank as an analyst before joining ADELA in 1972. A cool professional who would be sent on a moment's notice to run the troubled Brazil operation, Luis had a clear sense of the problem: "I became aware that while there was a complete *Investment Analyst*

78

Handbook of policy and procedure, there was none for credit analysis and procedure. It seems to me that maybe we could have avoided many bad loans with the proper corporate cash flow analysis procedures."

ADELA also lacked a well-developed system of funds management, which is the core of sound bank planning and financial management. Don Nicholson concluded that "ADELA got into lending, not banking, but never really understood the mechanics, hence it lent long out of short and had no base other than the somewhat expensive lines of credit it was given by shareholder banks and others." It remained for ADELA's last chairman, Bert Witham (IBM's treasurer), who signed the creditor's agreement that led to ADELA's liquidation, to summarize it: "Once we had started departing from many of our original precepts, that is that we were primarily in the business for providing equity and loan capital to new and expanding businesses, and got into the business of being more or less bankers without the capability of being bankers, we were headed for trouble."

To lend to small-to-medium businesses, ADELA needed to develop an experience-based capability to perform "due diligence" on new loan requests. Due diligence is both art and science. It is the art of asking hard questions and the science of testing the answers. It involves ferreting out basic information, clearly seeing potential risks, and then constructing financing suited to the borrower's circumstances. Turning loan requests into bankable propositions requires financial engineering: scheduling paybacks according to the projected cash flow, lending longer than the usual one to two years, and backing up loans with collateral such as the family home or land. To compensate for assuming greater risks than financial institutions are used to, the lender must charge equity-type fees (in lieu of owning shares in the companies). Neither international nor local banks are comfortable lending under that form. Thus, it represented a niche; ADELA could profit well by serving as a lender and simultaneously filling a pressing need in the local marketplace. But success depended on four capabilities that ADELA had not developed well in its first decade: knowing the customer and the customer's business, appraising the value of the collateral backing the loan, structuring repayments based on realistic cash flow projections, and closely following up to detect trouble, provide technical assistance, and reschedule when necessary.

ADELA housed the capability: it had in some part done this kind of business before. Some of its regional managers had ventured in this direction in various places. ADELA's Mexico City office professionals mastered these techniques in the second half of the 1970s, with impressive results. For a few years, until they were forced to stop doing new transactions, the Mexico office was profitable, had no new nonperformers, and no new defaults. They had learned how to execute, which is at the core of development lending. But for ADELA as a whole, the training of loan/investment officers via well-developed policies and procedures under vigilant, knowledgeable supervision had not been a hallmark of its executive administration. In fact, during Keller's second five years and under the board of management that he created, ADELA took risks that foreshadowed the "wild bets" that would bring down AIG, Citigroup, Shearson and Bear Stearns, thirty years later.

6. ADELA's Accomplishments

>~~<

The *Wall Street Journal* had portrayed ADELA as an investment company, capitalized with $40 million, that was bound to fail its developmental purpose considering Latin America's vast needs. By that standard, doomed also was the $100 billion Alliance for Progress, which by the early '70s was widely viewed as a failure. But the argument missed the point. ADELA was not meant to do it all. Rather it was to show the way and others would follow. Ernst Keller was undoubtedly right in proclaiming when he wrote me: "Its role and effectiveness as a developer of private enterprise in Latin America, measured against its own limited resources, has far exceeded that of comparable organizations, private and public." Senator Javits produced some interesting numbers in a letter to the *Wall Street Journal*: "Since its formation, ADELA has employed over $2 billion to implement its purpose. It has been instrumental in developing and expanding over 160 companies,....and has created employment for over 350,000 people."

In its first decade and a half, ADELA invested in 165 enterprises. Of those, thirty-eight failed outright or remained problematic. But that meant a 77 percent success rate (as measured by the venture capitalists themselves), which was certainly not bad for that kind of business in that place. In the more-developed U.S. market, an 80 percent success rate would have been the norm.

Moreover, ADELA showed good selection, execution, and supervision in many projects and investments. It contributed to economic growth by helping to create new jobs in new businesses and giving new players access to finance and technology. In its first years it reported having a "significant impact" on the inflow of long-term private capital by participating in more than $300 million (over $1 billion in today's dollars) of private investment in Latin America—much of it sponsored by ADELA. The $300 million would reach $2 billion (over $6.7 billion in today's dollars) in little more than a decade.

Soon after start-up, ADELA brought other development finance institutions into its projects. In its first year it showed a profit by bringing the region's largest financial player, the Inter-American Development Bank, into a joint investment program for $30 million. Also, it got another big player, the IFC, to make a parallel loan to an ADELA investee. Then ADELA got both institutions to join it in a large loan to a new pulp and paper project in Brazil in which ADELA had subscribed $3 million in shares. Moreover, ADELA later sold the pulp and paper investment at a handsome profit.

ADELA was certainly ambitious about getting projects moving. Investment activity was the main objective, as mentioned in every annual report. In its fifth year, for example, it increased its business volume by 170 percent over the previous year and proudly described its three main thrusts: as a provider of seed capital, as a mobilizer of funds, and as a one-stop financial supermarket.

ADELA offered to the region's businesses a full set of financial and technical services, accomplished with the collaboration of its technical consulting subsidiary, ADELATEC. Indeed, the latter worked with and for government and industry on major studies of tourist development, forestry, development banks, and other projects in several parts of Latin America, including the Caribbean.

ADELA's imaginative, energized investment officers produced some real winners. If asked for names, one could cite more than a baker's dozen:

Chemical companies in Nicaragua
Industrial park in Mexico
Beef exporter in Central America
Tin mining and dredging in Bolivia
Development finance in Colombia
Sandals and tarpaulins in Brazil
Bicycle manufacturing in Mexico
Textile manufacturing in Venezuela

Pulp and paper mill in Brazil
Leasing company in Brazil
LAAD, an agribusiness ADELA
Auto transmissions in Mexico
Finance company in Equador
Hotel in Colombia
Glass manufacturing in Colombia

The chemical companies in Nicaragua have already been mentioned. It is worthwhile to describe a few other investments to give the flavor of their diversity and importance:

Parque Industrial is an industrial park located on the Mexican side of the Rio Grande, in Ciudad Juarez across from El Paso, Texas. It was one of the first under the Mexican Border Industrialization Program to attract foreign industries to establish factories in Mexico. ADELA bought a 24 percent interest for $250,000 in 1970 and helped its owners, the Bermudez family, to develop it into one of the largest border industrial parks in Mexico. ADELA used its connections to find large foreign industrial companies, such as Electrolux, bring them into a lease-sale arrangement where the park would build to suit, hire and train workers, and eventually sell the building to them. With a contract in hand, ADELA's managers would cross the river to El Paso and negotiate with one of the American banks for a construction loan that would be self-liquidating through the lease.

The venture prospered, and eventually ADELA was able to negotiate a sale of its minority position to the Bermudez family, but it required lengthy negotiation because the local group was content with ADELA's participation. Meanwhile Mexico was caught in a debt crisis that ensnared all debt owed to foreigners. Nevertheless, ADELA's withdrawal was successfully engineered in 1983, thirteen years after the initial investment.

Agrodinámica was a vertically integrated, Central American cattle-raising, beef-processing enterprise. During ADELA's thirteen-year part ownership, Agrodinámica developed a major new dollar export, and helped advance the concept of Central American regional industries that were sized to compete in major international markets. Its four integrated cattle and beef complexes became Central America's largest beef exporter and leather producer and an important producer and distributor of dairy products. In 1980, as the company's annual earnings were peaking (at $3.3 million), ADELA sold its half, profitably, to the Costa Rican shareholder, Miguel Angel Rodriguez.

Latin American Agribusiness Development Corp (LAAD) was formed to be an ADELA for Latin American agriculture. ADELA bought 20 percent participation in LAAD, joining a group of sponsors from U.S. agribusiness-oriented financial, industrial, and commercial concerns. But its major contribution proved to be two alumni, Bob Ross and Tom Mooney, who led LAAD to fulfill its role as a financial intermediary for smaller private agribusiness investment in Central America and later in other Latin American countries. LAAD prospered then and prospers still. Founded in the 1970s with a small staff (which continues today) and an equally small board of executives from its twelve agribusiness shareholders, LAAD, nevertheless, has concentrated on a few basic loan products that it learned to do best and profitably. Operating in countries beset with political and natural tragedies, civil wars, and earthquakes, LAAD has managed to be consistently profitable and to pay back early support loans from USAID. At the end of the '70s, ADELA's financial condition forced it to relinquish its stake in LAAD.

Leasco was a leasing unit in Brazil, pioneered by ADELA and sold profitably to an ADELA shareholder bank. Leasing is a form of secured lending where the collateral is not a house or a piece of land but rather machinery and equipment *plus* an insurance policy on the remaining payments. It was and is a good way to be in the lending business: the collateral is easier to recover because it remains in the lessor's name. Leasco was great for helping small, young businesses that simply lacked the cash flow, capital, or size to qualify for regular bank loans or capital investment. For the ADELA shareholder bank, acquiring a leasing unit already operating in Brazil avoided the long and uncertain processes of gaining government permission to organize, of training the staff, and of finding the right niche.

Agrodinámica, LAAD, and Leasco are examples from a list of many successes, including a plywood factory and a sesame seed processing plant, both in Mexico, with local partners. Other ventures were scattered throughout ADELA's territory, for the company's investment projects were ubiquitous, numerous, and varied.

The achievements of ADELA's staff were indeed worthy of the company's promise. Their fault was in failing to provide the guidance and assistance to be more selective. They should have concentrated on fewer projects, where they could act as a catalyst bringing shareholders and local business groups together for important projects. The directors, reflecting their own, sponsoring companies' lack of interest in ADELA, overlooked this strategic concept.

Those managers who stayed and took over managing ADELA's troubled investments represented a very positive development. They had gained valuable experience that they put to good use. For example, Pete Collado had foreseen a big loss (more than $2 million) from the CTC lawsuit. ADELA's managers in the Mexico City office very imaginatively settled the suit favorably for both ADELA and the Mexican banks with which they had joined forces. The final result was that ADELA retrieved its $2 million loan and gained $600,000.

7. Governance, ADELA-Style

In graduate school, Professor Myles Mace shaped my view of the role of a board of directors. He taught that boards practice a few basic functions: setting policy, choosing the CEO, providing oversight, and asking "discerning" questions. And in crisis situations, they act. Demanding as that role may be, experience taught me that the board must do even more in a development vehicle. It must see to whatever nurturing and access to capital, technology, and markets are required to develop investments and eventually sell them off. Venture investment cannot be overseen passively like portfolio investment. It demands active director involvement. When operating with inexperienced investment managers in underdeveloped economies, this prerequisite becomes critical.

ADELA was not an operating company producing goods and services like its shareholder companies. It was a venture investing company in the business of finding, evaluating, and developing new enterprises. Its governance system needed to be organized around a small board— something like a partnership—with about half a dozen directors who would function like owner-members. Under them would be managers who owned no equity but could be incentivized to act as if they did by participating in investment gains when enterprises were sold. Both partners and managers had to know the venture capital business and be prepared to spend much time with each other and with the investee companies.

But the alliance of powerful international businesses that formed ADELA organized it in their own image as if it were a large operating company, or, more precisely, a business association. They went ahead with an outsize board of sixty-five, a number that would later rise to ninety-plus. The directors owned no shares in the business and often sent alternates to their relatively infrequent (for a venture investing company) board meetings. Top business executives had taken on the governance of a venture investing company when they had neither the time nor justification for paying quality attention to its affairs—even if they had known the business, which they didn't. Governance of venture investing companies differs significantly from governance of operating companies. My friend Pat Cloherty, then president of Alan Patricoff Associates, a venture capital firm, recognized these truths when she led a study of lessons learned from the ADELA experience. She concluded that ADELA's board "was far too large and institutionally mismatched for providing guidance on small entrepreneurial projects."

The story of ADELA's investment in Capsa is illustrative. Starting in 1966, ADELA invested more than $7 million in Capsa, a company located in Paraguay that processed cooking oil, cotton fiber, and tobacco. My banker/writer/friend Doug Villepique described the area: "Located on the muddy Paraguay River 1,000 miles upstream from Buenos Aires, the Capital, Asunción, had changed very little in over a century. At the time there was one traffic light in the entire country and only a few buildings over three stories tall. At noon, with the city shut down for siesta, stray dogs could sleep in peace in the middle of the main intersection." Hardly a place that would inspire extended visits from ADELA directors, like the chairman of the board of Esso or the chairman of the Bank of Tokyo.

Capsa got into trouble, and ADELA was forced to take over its management to protect the company's by then large investment. ADELA's CEO Keller told *Forbes Magazine* that he was proud of ADELA's ability to achieve turnarounds in such investments. "We could have lost $30-40 million by now if we had not had the fire brigade to send in," he said. He described the "fire brigade" as a team of one to five troubleshooters who move into a troubled company for six months to three years to iron out problems and turn red ink to black. "We had to step into Capsa when the majority stockholder became insolvent," said Keller. "After two years of hard work, the company is now earning in excess of 30 percent on invested capital." Sadly, the 30 percent return proved neither exact nor lasting. Having failed to properly size up the firm initially and to provide it with appropriate guidance going along, ADELA's top management had to put in a ton of money to save it, but it could not bring itself to acknowledge that the fix would not last.

A prominent Uruguayan family group with strong connections in Paraguay owned Capsa. ADELA had financed assorted deals with this group in Paraguay and in neighboring Uruguay. When problems piled up over questionable business practices, risky cross-border (country to country) trades, and off-balance sheet guarantees (i.e., liabilities not appearing on the company's balance sheet—as in the Bear Stearns imbroglio that was to come), the family members simply couldn't handle the business. ADELA's number two executive was sent in to sort things out and try to save it. He worked out a deal for ADELA to take over Capsa and then proceeded to bring in a stream of ADELA staffers to come to grips with what had become, in the words of an ADELA managing director, "the cash consuming monster ADELA had taken on." But the team proved unable to manage Capsa, so Keller brought in a Swiss turnaround artist who had successfully helped ADELA in a Mexican situation.

Within six months things began to calm down as Capsa's activities returned to some normalcy. By 1974 ADELA was in the early stages of a reorganization that would assign two ADELA managing directors to oversee Capsa. The second of the two was Don Nicholson, who had gained considerable business development experience with ADELA in

Brazil, where Capsa's trading activities were extensive, if not complex and murky.

Don realized that the operation was much too capital intensive and risky. In his own words: "I went to Pete Collado (then president of AD-ELA) and explained things. We agreed there and then that we had to get rid of Capsa and that was to become my main priority. Thanks to contacts I had we were soon in advanced talks with ADELA shareholder Continental Grain. After suitable due diligence we sold Capsa to them on July 19, 1977. The closing was in New York City, and I spent the night with a number of cashier's checks in my briefcase under the bed." Thus, in 1977, ten years after the initial investment, ADELA sold Capsa to Continental for a $2 million gain and in the process relieved itself of some $500,000 in claims. While this represented a 3.5 percent annualized return on investment, in truth it was before considering the cost of salaries and travel for the ADELA executives who spent so many years and so much effort on Capsa. Nevertheless, it represented a more significant achievement for ADELA than was generally appreciated. The $30 to $40 million figure mentioned by Keller as the potential loss seems to have been the actual amount that ADELA had at stake, even though its information system failed to show anything near this number.

Why did ADELA fail to bring this shareholder into the Capsa investment from the start? Why indeed did the ADELA director representing Continental Grain fail to take an interest in this investment from day one? Why did the board fail to fully appreciate ADELA's true exposure? The answers lie partly in the close-to-the-vest management style of CEO Keller, about whom George Moore, Citibank chairman, wrote: "When you asked him a hard question, he gave you a blizzard of facts from which you could never make even a snowman's worth of real information." But mainly it was in the oversight, or lack of it, performed by ADELA's board, as we shall explore.

By comparison, consider an agribusiness investment on another

90

continent, by the Bulgarian-American Enterprise Fund (BAEF), another venture investing company operating in a third-world setting. In that case, the CEO brought the problem to the board (ADELA's CEO would have kept it from them). One of the directors, knowledgeable in the business, took the lead to help the BAEF deal with the investee company's problems and at the same time build the board's comprehension.

The company was Ameta, a vertically-integrated poultry producer in Bulgaria in which BAEF had invested. In the late 1990s, BAEF's CEO told his board that Ameta was becoming a $6 million problem. The slaughterhouse badly needed repair; operating performance was below standard; management was weak; financial losses were large and increasing; and feed problems had surfaced. As a stopgap measure, the CEO replaced the manager with a young investment manager from BAEF. One BAEF director, a partner in an agricultural consulting company based in Washington, DC, began visiting the plant regularly. That was no easy hop; the plant was located in an interior region of Bulgaria, seven time zones from his home in Washington. He led an evaluation of the company and, most important, reassured the board enough to persuade it to invest the money to save it. In addition to assisting the CEO of the BAEF in rehabilitating and modernizing the company, he found a manager (located in the United States) with the skills and experience to complement the BAEF investment manager. Five years later, Ameta was hugely profitable with annual sales of $30 million. It was current on its loans from BAEF, and had paid back more than $1 million, which reduced BAEF's exposure to $5 million. When this was written, the loans had been repaid, and BAEF had sold the firm to the two men.

"As I reflect on the Ameta experience," wrote that director, "our principal strengths were in having a management that didn't attempt to hide the problem, and a group of directors who were willing to get directly involved to help solve problems when their experience was relevant." The director's active participation in the resolution of this problem investment was not unusual for BAEF. In another case, when legal problems began to loom, another director, appropriately a lawyer, stepped forward and assumed responsibility for successfully shepherding BAEF's defense in a lawsuit that eventually went to the U.S. Supreme Court before BAEF won.

Two more examples fill out the picture: When BAEF's bank began to grow into a major lending institution, one director with an international banking background assumed the chair of a newly formed banking oversight committee and began regular trips to Bulgaria with his committee to maintain close contact with the bank staff. Finally, as the group's real estate activities grew, still another director with considerable background in real estate activities took the lead in keeping watch and reviewing all the group's activities in that industry. As the group's real estate activities blossomed into a major activity, still another director, with considerable new venture experience, began educating us all about the business.

To followers of the downfalls of Enron, WorldCom, Tyco, Health South, and the like, corporate governance may seem an oxymoron. But *governance*, from the Greek for *steering*, was and still is about seeing that organizations are run right. ADELA certainly had directors capable of practicing good governance. As the company began, forty-seven of its sixty-five directors were chairmen or presidents of the world's leading international companies: IBM, Citibank, The Bank of Tokyo, General Motors, Esso, Deutsche Bank, Dunlop Tire, The Royal Bank of Canada, Coca-Cola, Ford, Swiss Bank Corporation, Fiat, Hitachi, Dow Chemical, among many others. The other eighteen directors were executive vice-presidents or managing directors of such companies and hardly less qualified. They all sat on their own boards, and on many others—commercial, philanthropic, and cultural. Evidently, they knew how to run and direct businesses and other institutions.

ADELA's founders chose to organize as a traditional joint stock corporation, with its capital held in stock shares. Venture capital groups are traditionally organized as partnerships, but the founders chose to accommodate several hundred participants in the venture. No shareholder could invest more than $500,000, which meant that no investor could hold more than 1 percent of the equity. They needed this restriction to avoid the impression that a few would control the many, or that those from one particular country or industry such as banking would be seen to dominate. (But, as mentioned earlier, the French, still fearing that the Americans would predominate, stayed out.)

This organization corresponded to the investors' needs. It followed their experience and practice in organizing consortiums in banking and petroleum. The organization style fit ADELA's situation particularly where more than two-hundred major corporations contributed funds to pursue a common goal. Although it belonged to all shareholders in this alliance, it lacked the leadership of a single entity or person. Once Senator Javits had brought them together and then stepped out, no one owned the project. This became evident in early 1980 when ADELA needed to recapitalize itself. Ernst Keller wrote me: "ADELA probably has the most prominent ownership of any company, a great asset in the fair-weather era 1964–1975. But ADELA has no real owners, and this is a grave disadvantage in difficult times as you are now passing through. A concentration of ownership would be desirable."

One person who might have taken the leadership was George Moore, whom Javits called his "apostle." Moore burst with ideas and activities. But he was then president of Citibank and getting ready to take on the role of chairman. Moreover, as president of New York's Metropolitan Opera, he was building a coalition of donors to fund the soon-to-be built Lincoln Center. And, as if to demonstrate the adage that the way to get something done is to hire a busy person, he had been corralled into helping Robert Moses pull together funding for the New York World's Fair.

Yet someone should have taken the lead in ADELA. The history and common sense of business alliances—actually any institutional alliances—shows that one of the partners must take charge. The ADELA project, particularly, needed leadership from the top to assure that its shareholding companies actively participated in its investment activities, that they brought their network of corporate relationships, capital, and capabilities into a partnership with Latin American businesses. Alas, it was not to be, which was unfortunate because board activism might have guided management as it navigated around Latin America. Leadership might have provided support in bouncing back from the adversity that would inevitably strike.

Actually, the chair and the board of ADELA never really set ADELA's compass. Both became rotating positions, with the chair characterized by EuroMoney Deputy Editor Tim Anderson as symbolic. Absent board leadership, management developed its own plans and went on about its projects while the owners passively awaited their completion. Down the road came consequences.

In the early 1970s the large, ninety-six-member Board of Directors morphed into a board of governors, which comprised all three hundred shareholders. The Board of Directors was then elected from that group according to a format that carefully mirrored the various constituencies such as countries, regions, and industries. The chair was selected from among them on a rotating basis—three years maximum. The peculiarity in ADELA was that the directors were mainly CEOs of their shareholder companies. The relatively miniscule investment in ADELA was not significant to their firms' success. Participating in a do-good alliance of world-class enterprises and their leaders was really related to peer pressure and prestige—for their companies and for themselves. Those "corporate chieftains," as one writer portrayed them, would see to it that participation on ADELA's boards did not keep them from their real work of running their own companies. That situation rendered it impossible for the company to effectively use its board.

That was no recipe for a successful venture. Adam Smith reasoned two hundred years earlier that the power of self-interest and the conflicts it generated made it extremely unlikely that a joint stock company could survive in any but the simplest of activities. One glaring example of the power of self-interest was the bank shareholders' opposition to having ADELA be a lender and in effect compete with them. President Keller saw ADELA's lending correctly when he stated that "much of ADELA's loans are just another form of venture capital, ahead of, and more secure than, equity investments." He made the point forcefully in a 1974 report to the Board of Directors in which he complained: "ADELA's weaknesses stem...in part from the reluctance of shareholders to let ADELA operate freely in activities similar to theirs." The problem of responsible oversight could have been fixed, but ADELA never faced the issue.

As I have said, ADELA's Board of Directors went from sixty-five in the first year and steadily increased to ninety-six in the fourth year. Obviously, this number was unwieldy, and so they formed an executive committee of eighteen, which was also unwieldy but continued growing until it reached twenty-nine in the sixth year. Those numbers flew in the face of wisdom. In the *Decline and Fall of the Roman Empire,* Edward Gibbon wrote: "The powers of sovereignty will be first abused and afterwards lost, if they are committed to an unwieldy multitude." If they forgot that history lesson, they might have remembered that their revered management guru Peter Drucker cautioned firms to keep boards small enough to be workable. As groups increase in size, they become less effective because the coordination and process problems overwhelm the advantages of having more people to draw on. Large boards are less vigilant and less decisive than smaller ones. In our own time, one of the world's largest, most complicated, and successful corporations, Microsoft, functions with a board of eight. Sony runs with nine. By contrast, ADELA's board, at the end of its first decade outnumbered staff, ninety-six to seventy-two.

Did ADELA's founders defy corporate practice in choosing such a large board and executive committee because they felt that the venture didn't need the tight control used for their own corporations? That ADELA would thrive with the looser oversight of the business association? Possibly, because many, when asked later for further capital support, said that they had paid their dues and had written off the investment. Much later in ADELA's history, as the *Wall Street Journal* noted, a new breed of chiefs who took over at many of ADELA's shareholder companies were looking more closely at their investment. Tom Wilcox, chief executive of Crocker National Bank of San Francisco said, "A half million dollars won't break me, but as a fiduciary, I've got to explain to my board why we're in ADELA." He became a leader in getting ADELA's board to face its deteriorated condition. But the effort was too late and too timid.

Two more anomalies fill in the picture: One was the frequency with which the chairmen succeeded each other; ADELA's first and formative ten years saw five chairmen. The second anomaly was the numerous resignations and elections of directors. Of the two dozen in the original directorate, eight lasted only one year, and another six lasted only one more year. Even after the fifth year, when board life could be expected to be a bit more routine, thirteen directors left and ten new ones came on. By contrast, at the Enterprise Funds, eight of the ten chairmen remained at their posts for fifteen years, and the other two were replaced only once during the period. But perhaps even more telling was the practice of ADELA's directors, including the chairman, to name permanent designated alternates to represent them at board meetings. By the fifth year, sixteen directors had designated permanent alternates. Even George Moore, chairman of Citibank, named an alternate. In a message to A. W. Clausen, president of the World Bank, he explained: "I think most of the top organizers like Citibank have abdicated for more important problems."

For example, Citibank had placed its investment in ADELA with FNOIC (First National Overseas Investment Corporation)—a catchall for the limited offshore investments that the bank was allowed to make in those days. The vice president in charge of FNOIC reported to a senior vice president, who in turn reported to the executive vice president in charge of the bank's overseas division, who in turn reported to the president of the bank. FNOIC's earnings target, set by the head of the overseas division, was to increase earnings by 15 percent per year. The comparatively small investment in ADELA could hardly provide the income that could help the division reach their target. Therefore, Citibank no longer cared about its ADELA investment.

To his credit, the FNOIC vice-president was a diligent member of ADELA's board, and he often referred ADELA projects to Citibank managers on-the-spot for their opinion. But ADELA's clients were too new or too small, and so they were often beneath Citibank's radar. Moreover, the Citi managers were great commercial lenders but inexperienced with equity investing.

Whatever reasons ADELA's directors had for failing to attend meetings, the lending banks noticed. Some voiced anger, some disgust. I'm certain the angst added to their punitive disposition toward ADELA when the company couldn't repay its loans. At any rate, in 1980, ADELA held two key meetings to discuss and vote on the restructuring plan and to discuss the Review Committee being imposed by ADELA's creditors. Alternates represented one-third of ADELA's directors marked as present. Imagine the absurdity of alternates discussing and voting on the Chrysler restructuring in the Iacocca era.

Could directors have named alternates at Citibank or Esso? I doubt it. Yet the practice became so notorious at ADELA that when it became necessary to call a meeting of the executive committee to consider ADELA's deterioration as revealed by an IFC review of the company's condition, Sir Reay Geddes, ADELA's chairman, had to be requested to "personally" ensure that the directors attend and not their alternates. Still, more than a few sent alternates, which rendered the meeting quite ineffective because representatives from Bank of America, Toronto Dominion Bank, and several Japanese shareholders, to cite a few, said they had to refer the matter to the home office. This effectively stifled consideration of alternate plans. For the chairman or CEO of a major company to designate himself as its director representative in an alliance and then name an alternate to represent him was to dodge accountability.

Another aspect of ADELA's board that greatly diminished its effectiveness was that it failed to become the kind of board that would challenge, question, or confront the CEO. Directors were especially reluctant to challenge CEO/President Keller, who was a very imposing presence, completely informed, according to George Moore. Moreover, Keller's supreme self-assurance was supported by consecutive years of growth and profits. "Annual meetings, held in different parts of the world, were elaborate affairs, sometimes more closely resembling conventions than meetings," wrote Tim Anderson in *Euromoney*. Those who could ask the hard questions were the alternate directors because they usually did their homework and tried to analyze the situation. Three in particular, Lindgren for Skanidavska Bank of Sweden, Ramaer for Philips of Holland, and Langton for IBM, were well-informed and deeply concerned. But, like the alternate director designated by George Moore, chairman of Citibank, they lacked the authority and prestige of those for whom they substituted. Also, they had no real stake in ADELA's fortunes. They attended to cast votes according to their sponsors' orientation, and to report back rather than to think forward. This procedure was a poor substitute for the probing discussions that should have been taking place at the board meetings.

One managing director excused the ADELA directors because "they were fed lies, half-truths and lots of misinformation." The investment in Capsa in Paraguay was cited as an example, where the administration "hid the real numbers and no one ever knew the full exposure." He said: "If you go back and read the ADELA annual reports, as I recently did, you'll see that the Capsa exposure was always hidden if not camouflaged.....The last thing wanted was to go to Continental Grain (an ADELA shareholder) or one of the other large trading houses, as that would have brought sunlight into things and ADELA's total exposure would have been revealed. Senior management was intent on distorting the facts...and accounting cronies in Zurich would doctor the books accordingly."

A senior manager held the view that the ADELA shareholders and directors never saw the company as a significant business enterprise geared to making a profit. Their investment was much too small ($500,000 maximum) to warrant much interest and dedication, and was certainly not expected to contribute significantly to their companies' profitability. "The main interest of ADELA's directors in attending board meetings was maintaining contact with one another. ....for them it was a nice way of keeping in touch or an opportunity to meet equally important peers from other companies or from other countries. Setting course and policy for ADELA as well as running ADELA was to a very large extent delegated to management. And there was very little control exerted by the board of directors on management." A quarter century would pass before board failures to curb executives' excesses, as epitomized by Enron, brought congressional overkill in the form of the Sarbanes-Oxley Act, and the new regulatory agency (PCAOB) it created.

Effectively organizing and overseeing a venture capital company appears to have been outside the experience of the ADELA crowd. Board size and composition definitely failed to correspond to the nature of the undertaking, as I have argued. ADELA was investing in new ventures or enterprises that were expanding into new areas. That kind of capital investing requires more than money: it requires that a small group, usually five to ten investors, manage and nurture enterprises.

They must have experience in mothering beginning companies. AD-ELA's president knew the investment business and Latin America well enough to provide guidance to his green investment officers. But as the investments multiplied and spread across the twenty-two countries of the Caribbean, and Central and South America, close guidance and control became problematic. The sheer number of investments, mostly in new or young ventures, reached 102 by the fifth year. They represented a total investment of $100 million—a lot of money in the '60s. Not only were the investments exceedingly numerous, important, and complex, they were also distantly located and ill-served by primitive communications. Equally important, neither the president nor ADELA's investment officers could provide what the directors could: access to people, markets, technology, and investment capital. Perhaps because they were managers of large-scale operating companies, they knew too little about the venture capital investment business. Perhaps the failure was that they were unfamiliar with Latin American countries. Moreover, they were much too busy running their own very large companies. As Professor Mace wrote: "The fact that the top executives of companies...are exceedingly busy people makes it unlikely that they can become deeply involved in another company's problems."

Simply stated, ADELA had the wrong set of directors to guide it. If the governors/directors had seen themselves as fiduciaries of their companies' investments, they might have bolstered the board with venture investment types. Or, taking a cue from the way their European partners practiced governance, they could have created a two-tier system that split governance into two boards: a supervisory board of shareholder representatives that monitored, and a board of management that defined corporate strategy and allocated resources. The latter could have been a working board that included people seasoned in venture capital investing. Unfortunately, ADELA's governors seem to have lost sight of this workable system so familiar to many of them who were Europeans. A small, working board or committee of people seasoned in venture capital investing and knowledgeable about Latin America likely could have provided the right direction and control. In contrast, a director of the Bulgarian-American Enterprise Fund (BAEF) said: "I suspect a strength of our board is that as a result of the commitment of the directors to the work of BAEF and their continuity in this capacity, they have come to know and respect the experience and skills of their fellow directors in a way that further facilitates director involvement."

ADELA had too many people involved in oversight, too many of the wrong type who were involved in running their own businesses and uninformed about ADELA's business. For example, in April 1979, after receiving a full report on ADELA's deteriorated situation and hearing proposals for reorganization, the board nevertheless turned to discussing two new major projects: one for investing in a Latin American leasing company and the other to found a South American finance company. Both projects were led by managing directors who would soon be asked to resign. So, in the end, the owners themselves failed ADELA because they bought their shares and put them away instead of giving ADELA the engaged oversight they gave their primary businesses. This may be anecdotal, but I remember calling on the treasurer of a large U.S. corporation during our campaign to persuade the shareholders to invest more capital and finding him unaware that his company owned ADELA shares. He said that the amounts were too small to show up in any reports he reviewed. Ernst Keller summarized it in a 1983 letter to me: "Later, during your time particularly, the board was no longer around to be counted. By then ADELA had lost its glamour and was handed down to second and third assistants. I agree in that ADELA's failure was all the way due to terrible failures in corporate governance." ADELA never inspired the board commitment that the Enterprise Funds enjoyed. Shareholder John Train thought it equally possible that the board lost interest in a failure. But I found that the board had not remained actively interested after the initial period.

One other aspect of the governance failure was how ADELA's owners (i.e. shareholder companies) conceived and applied their grand strategy. Founder Javits drew the big picture for them when he described ADELA's mission as helping to develop Latin America by applying private capital investment from the industrialized nations. It would be, he said, "an international investment company in which large business enterprises from many countries have limited financial interests." He saw ADELA ascertaining the private enterprise needs of a country and then assembling the deals to help meet them. ADELA would put up only a small amount of the funds for a new project. It would then find local entrepreneurs and other investors, negotiate for governmental approval and assistance, lend management and technical services, launch the project, and monitor its operation. To fill this crucial catalyst role, ADELA would call on the financial, managerial, and technical resources of its stockholders. "This method," Javits wrote, "encouraged the development of small business and local economic entities, which were often neglected and by-passed by traditional investors who put their capital in mines, huge agricultural plantations, and heavy industry." Not bad for a politician.

ADELA's chairman was on the same page as Senator Javits. Writing in ADELA's first annual report, he said that the company was "organized to make and develop capital investments in Latin America. Through its investment activities, ADELA could revitalize private enterprise by bringing in the capital and the talents of many enterprises in many nations into a partnership with Latin American businesses."

Thus, ADELA would be in the business of finding business projects in Latin America that could be developed with the application of money and know-how from its shareholders and then seeing to their realization. The need was definitely there to create exports that generated the dollars to pay for needed imports. Latin American governments were receptive to this approach, and ADELA's shareholders had the wherewithal to make it possible. Moreover, America's own development experience had been reaffirmed in the rebuilding of post-World War II Europe. Foreign capital unleashed in a receptive environment could be very productive. The blueprint was there. ADELA's board would have to see that it was followed. But to follow the vision of Senator Javits and its own chairman, the board would have to think through how the resources of big industrial world businesses, which were normally applied to big projects, could be applied to small businesses that were generally overlooked.

Achieving the mission would require a strategy that matched resources with opportunities. That meant tallying resources and then, based on the opportunities and obstacles, figuring how to apply those resources to reach the goals. ADELA's resources were the money, know-how, and market connections of its shareholders. The game would be to find entrepreneurs with the right projects to be developed with those resources.

Actually, more than a few large-scale projects requiring considerable development came right to ADELA's door. There were resorts in Baja California, Mexico, the Dominican Republic, and Brazil, to name just the larger ones. And there were huge agricultural projects including a 124,000-acre farm to be irrigated in Brazil's drought-stricken northeast, the 33,000-acre rice farm in British Honduras, big-scale cattle-fattening in Venezuela and Argentina, as well as meat packing. Both the larger and smaller economies offered industrial projects.

But ADELA's unseasoned field people did not yet know how to size up or develop projects or to bring in foreign partners. They needed to develop the good judgment that, according to an old boss, Walter Wriston, "comes from experience, and experience comes from bad judgment." In the meantime, for vetting proposed investments and also providing a technical service to Latin American entrepreneurs, Keller created AD-ELATEC, a technical arm that also would be a training ground for the analysts who knew next to nothing about business investing. It was one of those imaginative ideas that actually worked for a while in the sense that it helped develop projects and independently earned some fees. But it never really contributed to the vetting of investment proposals nor to the resolution of problem investments. Nor did it mobilize technical knowledge and assistance from shareholder companies to use for Latin American firms. Despite the extraordinary numbers trumpeted by management—570 assignments in less than a decade—ADELATEC failed to develop a strong fee business or even win support from the field managers. Moreover, it was never able to interface with shareholders, which was the real reason for its being.

This is not to imply that the strategy of working up projects for shareholder involvement could never succeed. It was a strategy that fit the circumstances of Latin America, and proved right for some managers, some of the time. In Central America, ADELA's Manager Tom Mooney used the concept to great effect by drawing into local projects know-how partners from international powerhouses of that time such as Intercontinental Hotels, Hercules Powder, Pennwalt, and Mitsubishi— none of them ADELA shareholders. The magnitude of the funding required the participation of autonomous local public development banks, so he brought them in too. This conferred the important advantage of facilitating the necessary government permissions and avoiding onerous restrictions. But the glue was ADELA's participation as minority shareholder acting as a "tie breaker," in Mooney's words, between the groups. One such investment, which he described as the most profitable single agribusiness ever installed in Nicaragua, was the Atlantic Coast Chemical Company (Atchemco), a producer of wood resin, turpentine, and pine oil. ADELA and the government development bank took over this company, an aging naval stores plant, after it got into difficulties. They reorganized it, buttressed it with U.S. capital and know-how, and reequipped it to work the thousands of acres of pine stumps in the sparse

Atlantic coast region to produce turpentine and pine oil for export. Credit Mooney for putting it all together.

Yet putting the strategy to work presented problems company-wide. As President George W. Bush's Defense Secretary Rumsfeld said: "...no battle plan survives first contact with the foe." The problem was that even if ADELA's managers had wanted shareholder involvement, the directors simply weren't there to connect the field managers with shareholders. The directors perceived oversight more in the corporate terms they knew, where management basically ran the show, and not as the close director involvement required for venture investing.

Few managers had Mooney's out-sized imagination for combining people and projects. He was a gung-ho, former OSS agent who had also been with the World Bank and the U.S. Agency for International Development. From experience in those official institutions, he had developed a broader, more realistic perspective on working in developing nations—meaning that he could see how to work with the public sector to overcome obstacles. But most of the managers responded to enormous pressure from the overpowering Keller to make investments by doing them with local individuals rather than with companies or investment groups. So they went mainly into small investments, one after the other. Although in the early years ADELA's astute CEO well controlled those investments, before long their number exceeded his grasp. The consequences are described in chapters 4 and 5, which discuss how ADELA carried out its activities.

One promising, if controversial, type of investment should have gained shareholder involvement and could have accommodated ADELA's small investments as well. That was to set up or invest in local development finance companies, or *financieras*, as they came to be called. Latin American *financieras* were like investment banks. They made loans and purchased equity (shares) in new or expanding industries. Those that were government-owned and operated as local development agencies had checkered histories. Many more were owned by private local groups and experienced the success-failure rate that would be expected of a new industry. Many survived, grew, and thrived. Two international aid agencies, USAID and the IFC, took a special interest in the *financieras* and gave them considerable financing. The political clout of those two institutions could be helpful to the *financieras* in gaining liberalization of currency and other controls from rule-ridden bureaucracies.

ADELA did actually invest in some of the *financieras*. A few went well, as in Ecuador, Paraguay, Bolivia, and parts of Central America, while others showed mixed results, as in Colombia. But overall, ADELA failed to make money on the *financieras* and found it difficult to get out of those investments. Moreover, ADELA's board didn't appreciate this kind of investment because it thought that ADELA would have to charge the *financieras* rates that would be too high for loans. That was shortsighted, because ADELA's shareholder banks could have made the loans directly to those *financieras* at most competitive rates. And through those *financieras*, ADELA's fledgling merchant bankers could have exercised and developed their talents for "doing deals." Appropriately supported by directors and shareholders, they could have arranged to bring money, know-how, or market connections to entrepreneurs and projects. And inside the *financieras*, they would have found colleagues who knew the local people and the markets. Just as important, ADELA would have had access to more professional staff for project vetting.

Keller had actually voiced a similar idea of doing the small investments through Adelitas (little ADELAs) to be formed with the participation of local financial groups, thus extending the reach of the regional ADELA manager. Keller's idea represented Senator Javits's vision of a rational way of achieving the "development of small businesses and local economic entities." And ADELA's banking shareholders should have been particularly interested because lending to Latin America was expanding and very competitive among large international banks. Participating in regional financial institutions could have provided a competitive edge. But Keller received little response from his Board of Directors whose bank representatives jealously tried to confine ADELA to non-banking activities. George Moore, chairman of Citibank, complained that "Keller tried to make it a risk capital international bank, over my objection, and fouled it up."

It is curious that, in those years, some of ADELA's shareholder banks followed Chase Manhattan Bank's beckoning into a consortium bank in London to channel loans into Latin America. That vehicle, Libra Bank, prospered for some years until the Latin American debt crisis of the early 1980s forced its liquidation. Meanwhile ADELA's shareholder banks were also pumping loans directly into ADELA. The proceeds of those loans went into long-term investments, thus laying the groundwork for trouble later when the banks wanted their money back and ADELA couldn't retrieve it. As a final word, ADELA's field managers, who had meanwhile developed little fiefdoms through their multiple small investments, were probably relieved that ADELA failed to invest in Adelitas.

As I have argued, we should not look for shortcomings in ADELA's strategic design, but rather in its execution and oversight. The right strategy for ADELA was, as originally conceived, to capitalize on its uniqueness—the roster of international shareholder firms that could contribute money plus whatever else was needed for developing business opportunities. ADELA might have formed investment vehicles with local financial or entrepreneurial groups to identify and develop those investment opportunities, which would have allowed it to gain instant local know-how and know-who and avoid the costly administrative and oversight structure needed to service full-fledged offices in each country. ADELA would have enjoyed fewer deals, but they could have generated shareholder interest and business that could have yielded dividends, capital gains, and fee business as well. If ADELA had followed that strategy, it could have fulfilled its promise. Instead, the directors chose to be AWOL.

8. Dealing with ADELA's Condition in the Late 1970s

When Pete Collado stepped from retirement into the CEO's job at AD-ELA in late 1976, he started to control the situation by moving the accounting group from Zurich to New York, where he was located. Then, to gain control of operations and deal directly with the field offices, he arranged for the departure of the three remaining managing directors. That was complicated, for he feared creating uncertainty among shareholders and lenders alike. He wrote fellow director John Phillimore in March 1978: "As we expected, the realization that they are not real candidates (to be CEO of ADELA) has shaken the three Managing Directors and this is unfortunately but not surprisingly impairing their operating efficiency and efforts."

Shortly afterward, I joined ADELA and began working with Pete on the central problem of many non-income-producing loans and investments that ADELA was carrying at increasingly higher interest. We called a managers' meeting in February 1979 in Guatemala City to update them on ADELA's situation and get them involved in its resolution. To my amazement, they could not believe that ADELA was broke.

Our plan was simple although exceedingly difficult to carry out: sell assets to raise cash and restrict new investments. It was difficult because selling dead assets at a loss reduced the company's capital and that in turn reduced its borrowing capacity. Worse, it pushed ADELA toward breaching covenants the lenders had established. Bravely, Pete took a hit for the year ending in June 1979 and reported a loss of $13 million. Then he resumed his retirement, and it fell to me and the team I was assembling, mainly from among the ranks of ADELA veterans, to carry on the turnaround without him.

New turnaround management

At ADELA's annual meeting held in Stockholm in October 1979, I took over as CEO and presented our new top management trio, with Ivor Davies, a Shell retiree, as chief financial officer and Rafael Morales as chief of operations. Ivor and I were located in New York City. Rafael and his operations group were located in Mexico City. Actually, the team had been running the operations for months and had gained a realistic appreciation of ADELA's situation. As a result, we were already into a drastic reorganization. At Stockholm we told the governors and directors that we had inherited a mess and had started cleaning it up. But changes in the environment were affecting our battle plan. The Iranian Revolution had provoked a record surge in oil prices (from $2 a barrel in 1973 to $30 by 1982) and another global recession with high international interest rates. Latin America was entering its "lost decade" of debt crisis, inflation, and devaluation in which almost all the Latin American economies collapsed after the 1970s. On the political side, adding to the difficulties, by that time all but four of the twenty-two Latin American countries were dictatorships.

ADELA's assets of almost $500 million were no longer solid enough to protect its debts of $400 million. Those assets contained over $150 million of nonperforming assets that were being carried mainly by borrowed funds. As the *Wall Street Journal* had reported, only 37 percent of the company's investments were profitable. The interest costs to carry the portfolio were causing losses that ate into capital. Real danger threatened that it would fall below limits set by ADELA's lending banks.

Therefore, we had drawn up an emergency plan that was already dealing with these issues. And we had some pretty good numbers to show for it. Rafael Morales, who had acquired a broad and deep knowledge of the portfolio and who was by then ADELA's senior VP in Mexico, developed a basic premise that, given enough time, ADELA had sufficient hard assets to pay off everyone. (Incidentally, he was the last one out the door when ADELA was eventually liquidated. And he proved his point.)

Our group devised a typical turnaround plan:

- A reorganization that centralized administration in New York City under our new CFO Davies and centralized field operations in Mexico City under the senior VP Morales. Authority was consolidated in a management committee composed of the three of us.
- A drastic reduction of expenses by closing the Zurich office, selling the headquarters building in Lima, plus the office floors in Caracas, Venezuela, and Central America; moving out of pricey Park Avenue offices in the Seagrams building to more modest quarters on Third Avenue; and reducing field offices and staff.
- An asset rehabilitation program that had a plan and a person assigned for each major asset.
- An increase of income to be achieved by collecting on the large amount of receivables and selling off loans and other assets.
- A moratorium on new investments until liquidity was normalized.
- Perhaps the key element, a capital injection from shareholders coupled with debt restructuring.

The governors approved the plan and the management team set to work. Our CFO referred to the plan as "equal pain for everyone."

An early test of our break from the past was the handling of a $1 million dividend in stock received from Bimex, a company that was listed (but hardly traded) on the Mexican stock exchange. Formerly, this dividend would have been added to earnings, but not this time. By contrast, in the five years from 1973 to 1977, almost half of ADELA's income (48 percent) had come from such stock dividends, according to the IFC. When ADELA stopped recording stock dividends as income, it depressed earnings by $6 million. Another practice we discontinued was to assume income from nonperforming loans even if it had not been collected for six months. ADELA's accounts receivable already contained $23 million representing overdue interest on loans that had long since gone sour. These amounts had been recorded as income but never actually collected.

The reserve for bad loans and investments was still another aspect of accounting that had become controversial. Keller was proud of ADELA's low loss record under his mandate, as he stated in a letter to the *Wall Street Journal* on May 9, 1978. But the numerator in the ratio of bad loans to total investments was kept minimal by a reluctance to recognize losses. Company policy established from the outset was that reserves should reach 15 percent of paid-in capital. Actually, ADELA violated this rule for seven of Keller's last eight years. Only in 1979, after Keller had retired and after Gonzalez and the Committee of Management had left, were the reserves adjusted to reality. At that time we doubled the charge and also wrote off $10 million of bad investments. Those charges against income resulted in a heretofore huge loss of $13 million for the year. It was followed in 1980 by a charge of $34 million, which was the main factor in the astonishing $50 million loss for that year.

Comparing methods for dealing with losses in the past shows how clean a break this was. Some years earlier, in a switch on the later Enron case, ADELA's external auditors Arthur Andersen challenged ADELA's charge of $5.5 million against earned surplus. If ADELA had charged the loss against income by setting up a reserve, its income for the year would have been wiped out, leaving the company with its first loss. When Arthur Andersen balked at Keller's practices, ADELA replaced Andersen with another firm that, curiously, was replaced by yet another in 1980 as a result of the IFC report. We might argue that the external auditors should have been kept and ADELA's Board of Directors replaced.

Our management team placed a moratorium on new loans and investment and established an operations office in Mexico City where Rafael Morales, senior operating officer, centralized the rehabilitation and divestment of the portfolio. We put programs in place for dealing with each asset. Here are two examples (more will be described later).

In 1974 ADELA made a loan to Textiles Ego, a Colombian clothing manufacturer. The company ran into trouble and the loan went unpaid. In 1980 we renegotiated and restructured the loan using funds that had been blocked under currency control rules. ADELA got a tight first mortgage on real estate worth 160 percent of the amount owed and recovered a significant amount of interest owed but not yet received. Out of an exposure of $344,000, ADELA eventually recovered $495,000.

ADELA's Costa Rican assets were blocked when banks in New York froze Costa Rica's accounts. Having previously collaborated with the government on development projects, ADELA used the goodwill it had built to persuade the National Bank to draw a check on an account in Panama for the amount of its frozen balances, $700,000. The check was hand-carried to Panama where it was immediately cashed. Then the funds were remitted to New York, thereby avoiding their being tied up in drawn-out rescheduling arrangements for Costa Rica. Had ADELA's management failed to act in this way, the deposits in Costa Rica might have remained blocked for five to ten years and then devalued. This incident was not singular. ADELA's management acted similarly in several places including Colombia and Brazil.

In Mexico, Fausto Garcia, Rafael's deputy manager, was winding up a very successful recovery of a bad loan to Bimex, which is worth describing, because the Mexico City office professionals would apply the strategies that he perfected in this case to revive and recover ADELA's large Mexican portfolio.

Bimex is a Mexican bicycle manufacturer, owned today by the Carlos Slim group and going strong. In the early 1970s, it was a public company listed on the Mexican Bolsa, but hardly traded. Control of Bimex was in the hands of the company Casasus Trigueros, which had pledged the shares to ADELA as collateral for a loan. I discuss the case, CTC as it was called, below. But here I want to explain what ADELA did with the shares when CTC went under in 1975.

ADELA's exposure of $1.9 million in CTC had been collateralized by shares representing 42 percent of Bimex. By the time CTC failed, Bimex unfortunately was almost bankrupt and had lost 68 percent of its equity. ADELA's shares were worth only $294,000. At that point Fausto was assigned to the workout. He was appointed chairman of the board of Bimex and proceeded to convince Bimex's lenders, which included not only major Mexican banks but also New York's Citibank, to convert their debt into equity. Over the next four years he advised the company on management, finances, and corporate strategies and, under his chosen manager, the company began showing profits again. With the oil price spike in 1979, the Mexican stock market skyrocketed and shares in Bimex reached record levels, allowing ADELA to sell out at a profit of $477,000. Incidentally, Fausto went on to become the principal owner of a quite successful investment company in Mexico.

In other cases, where negotiation couldn't succeed, ADELA instituted legal action, which became the mode with some thirty clients. Meanwhile, Davies, ADELA's chief financial officer, established tight financial controls and led negotiations with creditor banks toward a financial restructuring plan. To understand the dimensions of this effort, consider how ADELA had been funding its investments and the situation that resulted. When our new administration took over in late fall of 1979, the company owed some $351 million to its creditors. Two years later, it had paid back about half, or $177 million, and had reduced its debt to $174 million. Cash on hand amounted to $66 million, more than adequate to retire its bond debt and meet scheduled principal payments to the banks. Divestitures of equity investments had averaged one per month for more than two and one-half years, and collection or reactivation of nonaccrual loans had averaged almost two per month. Moreover, more than one-third of all nonaccrual loans were receiving some sort of payments, though not regularly enough to warrant active status by our now strict accounting standards. To give a measure of how adept the team had become at rectifying bad situations, let me recount the full story of the CTC loan.

The CTC loan

In 1972, two ADELA officials organized a $9 million syndicated loan to the Mexican company Casasus, Trigueros Y Compania. ADELA put up $2.5 million, and the rest came from American Express and six banks, three American and three Mexican. After the loan was granted, a series of irregular management practices and fraudulent situations caused CTC to become illiquid and default on the loan. Next came several years of litigation against CTC, disputes and conflicts between the syndicated lenders, and finally an American Express-led lawsuit against ADELA. The suit claimed that ADELA failed to tell the other lenders that it had studied CTC before the loan commitment and knew that CTC's founding partners had committed fraud and other irregularities, but that ADELA kept it secret because the two ADELA officials who did the study would be working for CTC and wanted the loan to go through. Actually, one of the American lending banks had been lending to CTC well before ADELA became involved and therefore should have known about the company's situation.

We inherited the management of this case in late 1978 and finally negotiated a settlement with all four American banks, buying their loans for fourteen cents on the dollar. We then negotiated with the Mexican government, which meanwhile had intervened with the three Mexican banks, to split the remaining assets. ADELA chose the Cuernavaca Golf Club property, leaving to the government the ownership of six Orange Crush soft drink bottling plants. ADELA received 65 percent of the shares in Cuernavaca, took an option to buy the remaining 35 percent, then sold it all for the full value of its exposure which, by that time, had risen to $3.8 million. The deal was for the buyer to pay $700,000 in cash, $2 million with a government-guaranteed promissory note (at good interest), plus the buyer's note for $1.1 million backed by shares in a Mexican hotel. That the buyer had been able to obtain a government guarantee, which very few people ever obtained, spoke well for the strength of the deal. Also, our management had favorable experience on the $9 million it had previously lent to the buyer. All things considered, including Mexico's economic/financial problems at the time, this was a pretty good deal. It showed again how adept ADELA's management team in Mexico had become at rehabilitating nonperforming loans and investments. It demonstrated also how the management team had learned to collaborate with the Mexican government in workouts of problem loans and investments. In this case, the cash plus government-guaranteed notes were sufficient to repay ADELA's exposure plus a $600,000 gain. That was the good news.

The bad news was that Mexico's economic and financial crisis continued to deepen; the peso was devalued 80 percent, and the notes had to be rescheduled. That was just when the Review Committee of the creditors took over and they, led by the IFC's representative, thought it imprudent to proceed without squeezing more from the deal. They wanted the buyer to pay down part of the note, agree to an escalation clause, and provide the committee with a personal financial statement that showed solvency, an impossibility considering that the buyer was illiquid. (As an aside, in the ten years that the BAEF group's bank in Bulgaria has been making loans, it has never sought the personal financial statement of a single borrower. The bank, which has been borrowing from the IFC all along, enjoys a BB Stable/B rating from Standard & Poors, and has maintained a loan loss record equal to or better than the top banks in the country. In 2007, *Euromoney* rated the Bulgarian-American Credit Bank as Bulgaria's best-managed company.)

Not only did the Review Committee members want solvency comfort from the individual borrower, but they wanted the government to provide more understanding about its guarantee. These requirements dismayed ADELA's management as much as the requirements on the borrowers, for fear that ADELA would suffer significant adverse repercussions in its future relations with the government. The Review Committee was second-guessing ADELA and asking for additional assurances, despite the fact that two of their members had never been to Mexico and didn't speak the language and all three lacked experience working in Mexico and dealing with the government. Moreover, they doubted that rescheduling had been properly negotiated and, furthermore, insisted that the rescheduling required no particular urgency. These stalemates continued while the situation deteriorated. That occurred at the end of 1983.

As I have said, when the turnaround efforts were well underway, the IFC review took place. Morales acknowledged that the IFC review had been "helpful because it analyzed what went wrong in ADELA," but it was misleading in that "it did not accept that the worst of the bad practices had been stopped." The IFC report failed to do more than passingly acknowledge that the record was already showing that management could recover and manage the portfolio. John Phillimore, the former ADELA board member and managing director of Baring Brothers, wrote me: "Attempting to solve the problem cases, which have of course multiplied considerably since my time and now evidently apply to all the territories in which ADELA operates, must be backbreaking work and the successes which [management] reports are truly remarkable."

In retrospect, I wonder whether ADELA's board had taken the trouble to read the company's 1979 Annual Report of six months earlier, which told of the transformation taking place. Certainly the creditors had not, because they led ADELA's shareholders into an unnecessary liquidation.

9. ADELA's Versailles

⌐⌐⌐

John Maynard Keynes made the case that the Treaty of Versailles ruined Germany. Similarly, ADELA's bankers in London meted out harsh terms that had the same result. I suppose the bankers would reply, as Calvin Coolidge famously did: "They hired the money didn't they?"

Recall that the IFC is a subsidiary of the World Bank created to finance private businesses in the developing world. In the 1970s, the IFC loaned ADELA $10 million. Late in the decade, three months before I became president, ADELA's Wilcox Committee, chaired by Tom Wilcox, chairman of San Francisco's Crocker Bank, asked IFC to look at ADELA.

IFC offered to critique ADELA, to study how they conducted business and how they made decisions. Wilcox told them that his committee had been set up to consider ADELA's future, but its current situation forced them to focus on the present. He explained: "you can't navigate because the ship is not floating." Pete Collado, a retired Exxon/Esso officer, was serving as temporary president and doubling as financial VP. The company had been without a chief financial officer for some time and was operating with the help of short-term loans because its portfolio of loans and investments was throwing off too little cash.

IFC went to Latin America in late fall of 1979 to study ADELA's operations. What started as a look at managerial control and future directions for the Wilcox Committee turned into an IFC inquiry into AD-

ELA's condition. That look produced strong criticism of ADELA's risk management plus the chilling finding that the company faced a critical cash situation that could cause its liquidation.

IFC found major problems with ADELA's investment policies and practices going back over seven years but sharply aggravated by exogenous factors. One was the high interest rate of 20 percent it was paying in the late '70s, up from 9 percent earlier in the decade. Another factor was the huge fluctuation in Latin American currencies as the region slid into its debt crisis. While those factors were responsible for almost half of ADELA's $14 million losses in 1979, the report concentrated on the endogenous factors in ADELA's situation having to do with risk management and staff work. IFC saw unsound practices stemming from the decentralized authority system that had allowed country officers to approve their own loans or investments without the usual safeguards. Lacking was a system of project analysis by trained staff accustomed to going outside for expert review of technological and technical aspects and review of projects by loan or investment committees and senior officials.

They cited the example of Nordela, a kyanite mine in Brazil. The IFC concluded that financial projections had been unrealistic and poorly done, that ADELA had failed to plan for overruns and failed to insist on complete plans for subsequent stages to show where additional funds would come from. Moreover, the IFC thought ADELA should have had an outside technical review. Instead, while ADELA fruitlessly pursued potential investors—thirty-five in all—the U.S. promoter abandoned the project. ADELA was left as the sole owner, plagued with labor problems. A decade later, ADELA finally satisfied its accumulated labor obligations by handing over the remaining property and equipment. It wrote off the investment, which by 1982 had risen to $951,000 from $42,000 a decade earlier. In the course of dealing with this problem investment, I contacted an old friend, Gils Allard, a professor of geology at the University of Georgia, who had worked for many years in Brazil.

He advised me to forget trying to do anything with Nordela. "You have to have certain parameters to get good recovery. There is an awful lot of kyanite in the world. Not all of it is economic to mine."

The IFC report said much about ADELA's failures of execution: it was unable to spot the right projects, vet them, guide investee companies, and review and control risk. Also, the report found that ADELA could not provide the cash for continued expansion of investments. But the IFC was talking history. The practices that led to the difficulties had already been stopped or corrected. ADELA now had good programs in place for recovering assets. Management just needed time for them to work.

Regarding deficient analysis of loan proposals and investment opportunities, ADELA's operations management responded: "As you are well aware we have for some time now implemented a much stricter analysis and selection process of loans. Results are reflected by the fact that practically no loans made over the past two years are problem cases." Regarding divestiture of equity investments, management added:

> We are implementing certain new portfolio management practices which we believe will allow us in the future to sell profitable investments at a capital gain. We continue reducing our total personnel and expect to finish fiscal 79/80 with a total of about 170 people as compared with about 210 today. Coupled with a reduction of personnel we have begun a program of cost reduction in many areas which will lead to greatly reduced operating expenses.

> Kompass in Brazil might be a good example of the type of mistakes that have resulted in the deteriorated situation in which ADELA finds itself today. It started out as a small "venture capital fund" investment and subsequently ADELA extended a $185,000 working capital loan. When Kompass was unable

to repay the loan, ADELA accepted to take the company over and become its sole owner. Subsequently ADELA increased its exposure to US$1,190,000 to "keep the company alive." During fiscal year 76/77 ADELA's equity investment of $751,000 was fully written off and during mid-fiscal year 78/79 ADELA's loan of $439,000 was also written off for a total loss of $1,190,000. The enterprise had proven itself totally unviable. ADELA should never have supported an unviable venture capital fund project (made at the sole discretion of an individual). But if it did, ADELA should have cut short its losses when the original loan of $185,000 went sour.

Rafael Morales, who headed the team, knew what he was talking about. He was the one who stayed on and accomplished the successful liquidation of ADELA over a twelve-year period.

Why wasn't the IFC taking these assertions into account? You have to go back to ADELA's formation to understand that ADELA had engendered much emotional hostility, especially from its shareholders. Neal Paterson, a senior executive of the IFC, provided some understanding. He was an old friend of mine from the time the IFC led a group of private banks to put up financing for Inco Ltd.'s $300 million nickel operation in Guatemala, of which I was CEO in the early 1970s. When I visited him shortly after joining ADELA, he told me that in the beginning the IFC was a candidate to become an ADELA shareholder. But ADELA's executive committee shot that prospect down. According to ADELA director Hague, one of the principal American bankers, it was a matter of religion or principle. Senator Javits, ADELA's founding father, wanted to keep the IFC as a lender and not as a shareholder because the shareholders felt that IFC would bring a bureaucratic approach to what was basically private venture capitalism. Whatever the reason, the IFC figured it out and later, when ADELA went to the IFC for a loan, it was tough to justify. In fact, Paterson said that two Central American directors voted against the loan.

Keeping the IFC out of ADELA was one thing; creating a rivalry was another. Keller told me: "In the first few years of ADELA, when Marty Rosen was IFC executive vice president, they did not like us at all. They had for a decade told their board that there were not sufficient projects around in the developing world, including Latin America. Then the newcomer ADELA found far more viable projects than it could handle and became a main 'supplier' to IFC." Keller actually published comparative figures when ADELA was in its ninth year—half as old as the IFC. His chart showed that in eight and one-half years ADELA had disbursed more than $1 billion, while the IFC in twice as many years had delivered only half that amount. Moreover, ADELA earned in its most recent year twice as much income as the IFC. So ADELA was larger, more profitable, and arguably having a much stronger developmental impact in Latin America than the government-owned IFC.

A former ADELA professional-turned-writer described the rivalry more picturesquely in a piece called "The Chickens Come Home to Roost." He wrote: "To ask the IFC to report on ADELA's possible financial and managerial problems was a bit like asking Cinderella's older sisters to express their opinion of her behaviour just after she had ruined her chances by slipping on the stairs, falling on the pumpkin, and breaking the prince's glass slipper. The IFC had always resented the almost magical aura that surrounded ADELA, with its magnificent list of shareholders, its speed in investing and its published success, as well as its ability to move decisively, free as it was from the bureaucratic constraints normal for a massive, public-sector subsidiary of the World Bank. Now the tables were turned and the shoe was firmly on the other foot."

Keller summed it up when he wrote me in 2003: "IFC always hated ADELA, except for the relatively short time when Bill Gaud (ex-USAID) ran IFC under McNamara and a close cooperation developed, with IFC participating in many larger projects we brought to them. McNamara and Gaud wanted IFC to become a shareholder of ADELA, a proposal which was (foolishly) turned down by the US shareholders as a group. Despite this, the IFC still approved some long-term funding for ADELA, but after Gaud had died of cancer and McNamara was gone we again faced a hostile attitude at IFC."

The IFC reported on ADELA in early January 1980, outside the United States–in Luxembourg. An IFC official rendered the report orally to a small group–the Wilcox Committee, which by then had morphed into a newly created Finance Committee, ADELA's chairman, and me. Why offshore and why orally? The official who delivered the report told me that it might be "libelous in half-dozen places. A slander or libel suit is probable." Checking with a valued legal mind, I learned that issuing the report in the United States could have exposed the IFC to defamation claims under U.S. law. Also, concern about the credibility of the charges may have caused IFC people to want to minimize the impact and import of the report by making it oral only and delivering it offshore.

At any rate, the IFC rep told us that they had been concerned about ADELA for two years and now viewed its situation as very serious. They required a clean break with the past in terms of the three remaining senior managing directors (actually all three had already departed), as well as the external auditor and the in-house counsel. They demanded three steps: reschedule the debt, establish a management committee of creditors' representatives to assist management over the next two years, and require shareholders to back the company with additional equity. The ultimate responsibility for the past, the IFC said, was on the governors and the board. If the board failed to respond, the IFC or some of the many creditors would pull the plug. They emphasized that if creditors were to accelerate–call their loans–they would pull down a house of cards.

The IFC report echoed our plan to emphasize asset rehabilitation, establish a moratorium with creditors, provide a capital assessment to the shareholders, and institute a three-person management committee comprising Morales (operations), Davies (finance), and me. But IFC's management committee would comprise outsiders who would make all decisions under a trustee arrangement, avoiding the courts. The IFC preconditions for proceeding came with a threat; as mentioned, they would expose ADELA if the board failed to accede. In lieu of the full board, which was unavailable by that time, ADELA's executive committee approved the demands.

Part of the deal was that the shareholders would add $50 million in new capital. As it turned out, they agreed to less than $20 million, part of which was impossibly conditioned. For example, Baring Brothers required that "the shareholders *all* put their shoulders to the wheel." A reason that more money failed to be forthcoming in response to our personal appeals was that many industrial shareholders read the situation as presaging ADELA's end. They simply would not contribute to a liquidation or wind down. The Swiss firm, Volkart Brothers, of which Ernst Keller was chairman, sent word that they "would be interested in seeing ADELA rebuilding the old activity," but were uninterested in "disbursing good money after the other, just for liquidation." The banks, it seems, had hurt the cause by spreading "the idea of only participating in the capital increase and debt restructuring plan in order to get their money back."

Then an unfortunately timed and highly publicized incident occurred at ADELA's Paraty resort development in Brazil. Dutch religious groups financed a group of squatters who accused ADELA of forcing them off the land they had occupied for years. Although ADELA was by then hopelessly mired in the development, the protesters demanded that ADELA stop dragging its feet and leave. The Dutch shareholders were spooked.

The IFC attitude and the Paraty incident limited our options. Thus, ADELA's directors never seriously considered declaring bankruptcy.

Too many shareholders, especially European shareholders, wanted out with a bit of honor. Moreover, fear swirled that the banks could file for involuntary bankruptcy and take over the company on the grounds that it had concealed from them its true condition.

The deal with the lenders

In January 1980, we met twice in London with all our creditors to inform them that, in view of the company's illiquidity, ADELA could not meet the payment schedules and needed loan restructurings. Some of the creditors chided the few ADELA directors who were present: "You fellows can run the biggest company in the world. Why couldn't you run this one? You were negligent, that's why." That set the tone. At Versailles, the defeated faced just one Clemenceau. ADELA encountered a gaggle seeking retribution. The creditor representatives took the IFC plan as their own and made it even harsher. Having lent prodigally to Latin America during the '70s, those international financial institutions were now scrambling to cut back and get out as the Latin American debt crisis deepened. Their punitive mood reflected a feeling that ADELA's rich shareholder parents should pay for their child's transgressions. The Philips International director wrote to other Dutch shareholders: "My general impression was that the creditors realize fully that under the present circumstances in Latin America there is no choice but to agree on the flexible schedule. Surprisingly enough one of the few partners that is making difficulties appears to be the International Finance Corporation."

The IFC report provided the catalyst that closed shareholder minds. Unfortunately, ADELA's Euro shareholders widely shared the feeling that ADELA should be dealt the coup de grâce, and many among the U.S. industrial shareholders felt the same. Proof that very little interest remained in keeping ADELA afloat came when our request for a capital injection produced only $20 million, not the $50 million the creditors sought. Many subscribed only on the basis of an orderly liquidation.

The angry creditors turned the meeting into an interrogation. The IFC representative accused the ADELA shareholders of failing to come up with enough new money. The ADELA director representing Exxon/Esso was roundly criticized for coming up with only one-third of what the creditors expected from his company.

Anger turned to rage when the matter of rescheduling ADELA's bonds was put on the table. One of Gonzalez's first acts in 1976 when he succeeded Keller was to issue a $25 million floating rate bond in the European market using shareholder Baring Brothers as the lead underwriter. No one then had thought about the consequences of going outside the family for financing, but now the repercussions came back to haunt them. The bonds were about to become the first publicly listed Eurobonds ever to be rescheduled. Euro bonds, incidentally, were issued in U.S. dollars and sold by banks and other financial houses to investors throughout Europe. The bonds paid interest and principal according to a fixed schedule. Eurobond payments had never previously been rescheduled, that is, postponed.

Tim Anderson, writing in *EuroMoney* in September 1981, said that the banks forced rescheduling in an attempt to salvage something from the $240 million they were owed. Possibly they thought the ADELA shareholder parents might come through and pay the notes to save their reputations. If so, they misread the mood of the ADELA shareholders, who were unwilling to throw their good money after bad. Anderson called the event "the violation of the bond market." It was, after all, the first Euro-default in a heretofore unregulated free-form bond market. The effects would be felt for some time until the participants and their memories faded from the scene.

As the talks went on, the creditors' representatives and their lawyers were doing the talking, and it became obvious that we were there just to be talked at. They offered no acknowledgement from their side that ADELA's problem was illiquidity that had been produced by borrowing short term and lending/investing long term. And now, because of the Latin American debt crisis, ADELA could not sell off assets. The creditors would not hear our argument that enough hard assets existed to pay everyone off with time.

At one point, when we questioned the intended effect of a certain provision, a syndicate leader blurted: "We are not talking about ADELA's future, we are in liquidation."

Interestingly, one of ADELA's shareholders and creditors, Continental Illinois Bank, which had been aggressively lending to Latin America through syndicated loans, also suffered a liquidity squeeze at the same time. The potential losses were so high that the bank was judged "too big to fail." The Federal Deposit Insurance Corporation bought its assets, absorbed the losses, and turned them back to the bank to work them out. Once this was accomplished, the bank was sold to Bank of America in 1994. At the same time, another deal was struck with creditor banks to restructure the debt of the Sandinista government in Nicaragua. The deal deferred payment of interest and principal over a twelve-year period, rather than the normal five to seven years. The banks at the table with the Sandinistas included many at the table with ADELA.

The impossibly unrealistic arrangement that was forced on ADELA provided for a five-year restructuring of the debt, but ADELA had most of its loans and investments in Brazil, Mexico, Argentina, and Chile, which were all in crisis. Contemplating a ballooning of Citibank's cost of carrying debt, George C. Scott, senior credit officer, commented: "There was nothing a 6 percent rate cut wouldn't have cured, but the banks wouldn't get together." Instead, more ominously, a committee of lender representatives, now to be called the Review Committee, would in effect manage the company. This committee imposed onerous conditions such as "rolling up" (deferring) any interest over 8 percent for payment either from profits or capital, the legal consequences of which would threaten the very existence of ADELA's parent/holding company in Luxembourg, as well as its lending arm in Panama. (Incidentally, the IFC was the only beneficiary of the restructuring. Their loan was at a fixed rate of 9 percent. All the others were at Libor (8 percent) plus a floating rate. The floating rate part was rolled up to be paid with preferred stock. Since the IFC's loan was at a fixed rate, none of the interest ADELA owed it was rolled up. They received their regular interest rate just as before.)

This foolish condition obliged the company to seek offers as speedily as possible for its investments, at a time when Latin America's economic and financial problems were beyond serious: gold was hitting $800 an ounce, up from $400, and interest rates had reached 20 percent. Two years later we returned to the table with the creditors for a second rescheduling, and still later a third, because economic conditions in Latin America prohibited the asset sales and recoveries at the pace the agreement required.

The Review Committee tied our hands until the creditors abandoned it at the end of 1983. This was ADELA's second experiment with management by committee. The first occurred when Keller left and a management board of four managing directors with equal powers was established, with a following disastrous power struggle. The second experience, decreed by the IFC with the creditor banks, was fatal. It is said that many New York law firms have gone bust being run collectively, because you cannot manage by committee. Certainly never in a crisis. Peter Drucker has explained it clearly: "Someone in the organization must have the authority to make the final decision. Without that authority, the organization could be paralyzed or unable to deal in a crisis situation."

Management by Committee: The Review Committee

David Ogilvy, chairman of Ogilvy & Mather of Madison Avenue, wrote: "Search your parks in all the cities, you'll find no statues of committees."

Former CEO Keller wrote me on June 6, 1980, after learning about the establishment of the Review Committee:

> We continue to question the need and wisdom of "management by committee." Firstly, any emergency requires clear and ample authority for taking decisions, and ADELA's present situation is without doubt an emergency. Secondly, even in previous more normal times ADELA needed "handson management" in the places where its opportunities and problems were. Both the nature of its business and ADELA's present situation do not allow for management from an executive suite, and much less for management by committee.
>
> Any such committee, whether advisory or supervisory, is in our view undesirable and an additional hindrance for an already most difficult task. It would tend to blur responsibility and authority which must clearly be yours. We also doubt whether the shareholders, creditors and IFC are prepared to make some of their highest caliber men available for any length of time, as the situation would require. And a group of frightened "funcionarios" trying to exercise a decisive influence on management and activities could easily be the kiss of death.

How prescient!

The Review Committee cost ADELA $350,000 each year, an amount one investment banker characterized as "outrageous." This was on top of the almost $500,000 the banks charged ADELA for the "privilege" of doing the first restructuring. The committee's three members included a former banker representing the American bank creditors, an official of the German Dresdner Bank (a shareholder and big ADELA creditor) representing the skittish bondholder agents, and an IFC representative. The first was independent, the second deferred to the IFC rep, and the latter acted as if he were the whole committee, with full powers. From day one, the relations between ADELA's management and the Review Committee were difficult and never got better. The IFC representative was openly contemptuous of management and absolutely convinced that he had to see, revise, often negotiate, and approve every action taken to recover assets. His insatiable demand for memos from the field managers was matched by his own production. It should be no surprise that his visits to field offices aroused ire, demoralized staff, and undercut senior management. Consider a complaint from Brazil: "He came here as the manager of ADELA. He gave the impression that he or the IFC was running things...that he was personally intervening in Brazil because he couldn't trust senior management."

In another instance, of many, our CFO had to tell him that counsel retained to file a lawsuit on our behalf "seem to have the impression that you are handling this case for and on behalf of ADELA." In other words, it seemed as if ADELA had contracted him to represent their interests in this case.

Never mind that the documents said that the committee was to "monitor adherence to the approved financial plan and ensure an information flow to the stakeholders." Nor that Dr. Frankel, the board member from Dresdner Bank, voiced concern that "the Management Committee not contravene the common sense of how a corporation is run." In practice the committee preempted management, and his man on the committee was one of those who did so. In taking over, the committee seriously corrupted management's ability to hold the organization together and recover ADELA's investments.

ADELA's chairmen during the period, Sir Reay Geddes, deputy chairman of Midland Bank Ltd, followed by Bert Witham of IBM, fretted that the committee was preempting management, but they took no action. The executive committee early on expressed its support for my efforts to make the Review Committee workable and made some effort to reign in the three members. Others tried to intervene directly on our behalf, including Citibank's recently retired Chairman George Moore, who wrote to his friend A. W. Clausen, president of the World Bank. The result was counterproductive. The bureaucrats at the IFC closed ranks around their representative, and ADELA was worse off than before.

The situation became so strained that at the annual meeting of ADELA's governors in Toronto, in October 1982, Rafael Morales bluntly told them that the decision-making process had slowed to a crawl: "Every decision, no matter whether important or immaterial, has to be approved by the Review Committee prior to implementation; all authority has been stripped from our field managers, with the result that we have lost a number of our best men during the previous eighteen months, just when we needed them most; and an inordinate amount of time has been spent by our operations people in reporting and clarifying questions from the Review Committee." The governors listened, and that was all. Meanwhile, ADELA went on losing staff and opportunities for recovering bad loans and investments.

Actually, Morales was understating the case. Not just field managers but clients as well perceived that the committee, or at least one member, was running the company. He could have cited several cases where ADELA lost a divestiture because of the Review Committee's delay or interference. Here are just four examples:

■ The Swissmex Investment in Mexico: Morales had been preaching about the overvalued peso and urging a quick sale.

But the Review Committee insisted that the shares be sold at ten times earnings, so the sale did not go through. Then came the devaluations when Mexico defaulted on its debt in 1982, and the opportunity was lost.

■ The industrial park in Mexico: We didn't lose the restructuring, but the episode cost us in our relations with the majority shareholder, and we lost the opportunity to work out a deal for selling our shares. ADELA had to wait another three years before realizing a sale.

■ Sale of the office floor in Venezuela: If the Review Committee had not pressured management to seek another, more formal valuation, the whole floor might have been sold six months earlier. While waiting for ADELA to find a satisfactory appraiser, the buyer backed out. The result was that ADELA later sold only one-half the floor.

■ ADELA's treasurer in Zurich ran into the Review Committee's stone wall when he tried to take advantage of a strengthened dollar to purchase Swiss Francs to meet a payment coming due in six months. His letter to me is eloquent in its stiff Swiss syntax:

Reference is made to our tel. conversation. On July 10, 1981 we handed over to you and R. Kennedy [member of the Review Committee] a calculation regarding cost impact of purchasing Sfr. with dollars and the related interest loss on lower yielding Sfr. time deposits. This presentation was made at your request in order to enable the Review Committee to make a decision with respect to my request for approval to purchase the Sfrs. we were missing to meet the December 81 maturity, taking advantage of the dollar which at that time was becoming stronger and stronger. The decision of the Review Committee must have been mistakenly advised, since my request was turned down and no approval was given. By doing so the Review Committee has not only made the company lose the opportunity to save over US$600,000, but it has also left the Zurich office with the strong feeling of not being adequately understood by those who, as is supposed to be, should strengthen the financial side through fast and wise decisions.

The second, no less detrimental, decision had been taken, surprisingly, during the absence of the undersigned in military service when Zurich was unauthorised to go beyond the 1 month term for placements of time deposits. This erroneous decision, in contradiction to discussions and guide lines worked out at the beginning of the year with participation of all parties concerned, was taken at a time when the market rates were still quite high but signs were clear that the tendency was and would continue to be in the very near future a downward trend, hence providing less income for the future. The impact was so disastrous that ADELA lost an interest income of approximately US$12 million.

The above two losses are hurting the ADELA group very much at a time when, on the other side, the New York office Review Committee is charging petty items on the Zurich side, spending on telexes and telephone calls amounts which are well above the US$50,100 of the income which could eventually have resulted.... One must arrive at the conclusion that looking at the many trees New York cannot find the forest.

His frustration led him to resign soon after.

Robert Kennedy, the Review Committee member representing the U.S. banks, finally wrote to the creditor banks:

As far back as January 1982 I informed certain members of the Steering Committee that I sensed my position on the Review Committee would prove most unusual. The other two members of the Review Committee, namely the representative of the Dresdner Bank, A.G. and the representative of the IFC viewed their function quite differently than I. I was always under the concept that the Review Committee was not to interfere with Management but was there to help and assist them in their efforts to maximize the recovery from the ADELA Group for all interested parties. I quickly realized that this was not necessarily the case and events that transpired going forward more than bore such conclusion out. I suggest that each of you look to where ADELA is today relative to where it was three years ago......Some very positive things have happened and some good things will happen in the future.

Failing to receive the response he sought (namely, dissolving the Review Committee), he resigned and was not replaced. Actually, there was a muted response. One ADELA director, the senior managing director of a major European banking house, wrote: "I am wholeheartedly on Mr. Kennedy's side." But no one heard him. Ernst Keller reentered the fray with a letter to ADELA's chairman:

> As to the threemen review committee I had advised Joe Borgatti strongly against accepting such an arrangement after I had listened to the presentation of the rescue plan made to the Swiss shareholders in Zurich. Any such arrangements are fatal, particularly when a company is in trouble. Strong leadership, excellent management with clearly defined responsibilities and authority are the elementary requisites for dealing with troubled compa-

nies. Bernardo Quintana (Vice Chairman of ADELA) told me some time back about the untenable situation this threemen group had created. My reaction was that if I were the chairman, a. director, or the president of ADELA I would ask the creditors to decide who should bear the responsibility for running the company, the board and management or the threemen group appointed by them. If they want the threemen group the board and management should resign. If they want you, the board and management to stay I would insist that they withdraw the three-man group. In Latin America I have heard a great deal about this group, specifically about the IFC man on it, who seems to behave as if he was running ADELA. If so, why not let him? I suspect that these three fellows would be withdrawn real fast if you and the board and management would lay it on the line.

So much for turnaround management by committee. Surely the creditors, if not the board, should have known that a committee cannot manage a turnaround. In a crisis, as Peter Drucker argued, someone must clearly be in command. Survival depends on it.

If ADELA's creditors and shareholders failed to see the company's value, many others wanted to take over and work off its assets, for a fee. Among them was an ex-IFC official who had just left that institution. Another was a former executive of one of the leading creditor banks. Both gained the interest of ADELA's board and of the creditor representatives, but in the end they and others were summarily rejected. I have always thought that they were rejected because ADELA's field staff expressed strong misgivings. They feared that anyone who came into ADELA would be likely to tear it apart for whatever salvage money they could get. They would cast off ADELA's staff once they had used them to accomplish their plunder.

Nevertheless, despite the albatross of the Review Committee, our management group reduced ADELA's debt to the banks by two thirds. But as Latin American economic conditions worsened, the lenders twice again forced ADELA to restructure its debt, each time with unrealistic, if not onerous conditions. In mid-1983, based on management's record of having recovered more than $230 million from assets, and having paid creditors interest and principal amounting to more than $360 million, I formally asked the company to allow me to manage without the shackles of the Review Committee. I also proposed reducing the board to seven members, including creditor representatives, remunerating the chair position, having the chair monitor compliance with the restructuring agreement, and allowing management to do the managing, but with set targets and accountability. The executive committee gave no formal response. Finally, toward the end of 1983, as the economic and financial problems of Latin America intensified, the creditors pulled the plug and forced ADELA into liquidation. At year end, the board asked me to leave and entrusted the liquidation to Senior Vice President Rafael Morales, overseen by Ivor Davies who took over as president for a few years. It took Morales fifteen years, but he paid back all the loans. The lenders lost only their interest. The shareholders had lost theirs much earlier.

10. Conclusions

>᠊᠊

ADELA was founded on the idea that private capital and know-how from the industrial world would aid in developing Latin America's private sector. The dream started fading the moment the investing shareholders put away their checkbooks. Many of those corporate investors never meant to do anything more than contribute to a noble charity. Some wrote off their shares soon after they bought them; others followed later. Without shareholder involvement, ADELA's original mission was rendered impossible. And the company's club-like board arrangement impeded vigilant oversight. Left unfixed, those structural deficiencies became major causes of ADELA's decline and fall. Two other types of causes—situational and psychological—complete the story.

Structural causes of ADELA's decline

ADELA's business model was to create joint ventures by matching shareowners' resources and needs with those of Latin American businesses. Reaching their goals happened only occasionally because the Board of Directors provided a weak link between investors and AD-ELA's managers in the field. Board members rotated too frequently to fulfill their role, and part-time chairs led uncertainly. The directors seldom ventured out to meet with the field staff and see the investments firsthand. Given their day jobs as operating executives of major corporations, they could not have been expected to do so. So they never really knew ADELA's business, what its young managers were doing, and which projects could be paired with shareholders. This inappropriate oversight structure meant that ADELA's directors provided no real company governance. They failed to match the resources of ADELA's shareholders to management projects, so shareholders were not interested in or not informed about opportunities. Directors never tried to develop an alternative workable business model. Their neglect left management pretty much on its own. Managers had no power to get shareholder investments, so they did the next best thing: they borrowed money in the U.S. and European markets on the strength of the shareholders' names. The banks were only too happy to lend to a company owned by 240 of the largest industrial and financial companies.

Situational causes

When CEO Keller abruptly departed, he left behind a dysfunctional senior management group that was unable to control the problem that so many of their loans and investments were under-performing or, in many cases, nonperforming. Meanwhile, the surrounding political and economic conditions were deteriorating. Although ADELA's Board of Directors had not intended to fail the company, their negligent oversight fostered poor risk management, which in turn caused the company to slide into a liquidity crisis. ADELA's outside creditors, spooked by the deepening Latin American debt crisis and unable to force the shareholders to pay for their offspring's transgressions, over-reacted and forced the company into liquidation. If this story has any surprises, it is that the creditors expected ADELA's shareholders to behave more responsibly than they themselves did.

Psychological causes

A final strand must be woven into an understanding of ADELA's misfortunes, a factor that has been used to explain the failure of judgment in companies such as Enron and WorldCom. Certain psychological tendencies foster poor decision making. Jimmy Cayne, the head of Bear Sterns investment bank comes to mind. A quarter of a century after the ADELA failure, he went off to compete in a bridge tournament as his company neared collapse.

The directors who came together in ADELA's board room were high-powered leaders of the world's largest corporations. They knew how to make big decisions and run big enterprises. Their confidence in their ability would have been reinforced when they looked around the room at each other. This powerful self-view provides the best explanation of why they never assessed the Latin American environment before plunging in, why they never tried to understand the business, and why they failed to perceive the risks ADELA was taking until it was too late.

ADELA's directors and governors likely over-estimated their ability to discern and resolve problems. Like them, if not more so, the CEO had no doubts about his own abilities and served to reinforce their over-arching sense of self-worth. With this supremely self-assured skipper at the helm, and enthusiastic reports coming in from the company, the directors sailed along on the buoyancy of the seeming profitability of their very expansive venture. This is reminiscent of our confident, strong-minded defense establishment in the McNamara era. John Kenneth Galbraith, in *A Journey Through Economic Time*, wrote that the conduct of their Vietnam War "was the product of the most professionally accomplished of error."

ADELA's strategic purpose required that shareholders would play much more active roles than was customary in typical corporations. When that failed to happen, the Board should have devised a different strategy. But shareholder disinterest left ADELA with a revolving door to the board room and no real leadership. Under that structure, the Board neither strategized nor supervised. When the Latin American debt crisis deepened, the shareholders could not unite behind management's effort to work out of the liquidity problem. Instead, they allowed the IFC-led creditors to push ADELA into liquidation.

What can we finally say about ADELA's rise and fall? Acting responsibly, international business concerns created ADELA. But, as with any investments, ADELA needed to be looked after. By treating their contribution not as investment but as charity, the owners tarnished the deed and planted the seed of failure.

11. Lessons from ADELA

⤚⤙

Does the ADELA experience offer lessons to be learned? The consulting firm of Tesler & Cloherty didn't think so. Their study concluded: "ADELA is for the most part an untold story which would take great efforts to reconstruct in detail, without much value added." The firm concluded that investors could not have made money investing in shares of Latin American companies under the conditions prevailing at the time, and certainly not the way ADELA did it.

History proves them right, but that does not preclude learning from the mistakes. Just as important is learning about what could and did work for development investing. The ADELA experience says a great deal to investors who are returning to Latin America, or who are investing for the first time in Africa, Eastern Europe, and Asia. Moreover, its lessons go to the very heart of management practices: purposes, goals, strategies, governances, and alliances.

About venture investing: To develop a core business, a venture capital enterprise must use a strategy that aligns its strengths to opportunities and obstacles. ADELA's distinctive strength was its shareholder base of large international companies with plenty of money, know-how, and market access. The right strategy for ADELA would have been to capitalize on this unique shareholder base by developing business opportunities for them. Projects to develop exports from Latin America to the industrialized world would have capitalized on the position of AD-

ELA's shareholder companies in the world's markets while mitigating exchange risk. Such projects would have found favor both with local business groups and governments because they could generate much-needed hard currency. Also, they would have presented ADELA with chances to engage with government financial institutions and develop the collaborative relationships that proved so beneficial to ADELA's Mexico City office. Finally, such projects, by being larger, fewer in number, and more broadly backed, could have avoided four pitfalls that ADELA fell into:

- being a minority investor and being stuck inside with no voice in decision making
- going it alone with no other investors following to share development costs
- having insufficient know-how, know-who, and capital
- investing in far too many ventures to monitor and nurture appropriately.

ADELA could have brought its financial shareholders into investment vehicles, the so-called *financieras* formed by local financial groups and favored by international aid agencies. The *financieras* could have identified and developed opportunities. ADELA would have gained instant local know-how and know-who, and would have avoided the need to form costly administrative and oversight structures for servicing full-fledged offices in each country where flocks of sibling ventures were operating. They would have avoided getting locked into minority holdings. Also, the *financieras* tended to favor loans rather than equity investments, which means that they would have been an object lesson for weaning ADELA from the equity-based model.

ADELA did go into some *financieras*, but it failed to bring any of its 79 bank shareholders in as lenders or any of its industrial shareholders as equity investors. Many of the *financieras* had good pay-back records, and offered attractive opportunities for collateral business. How much more productive this approach might have been for ADELA's banking shareholders than lending to governments and government-owned companies. Yet, fatefully, ADELA's banking shareholders chose to compete with one another and with the rest of the international lending pack to push loans to the government sector throughout Latin America in the 1970s. And they all paid a price in huge write-offs; they got back centavos for their dollars.

A second lesson for venture investors is to begin operations in new settings by first financing expansions of existing firms. Doing a series of such projects builds investing capability and confidence at relatively low risk while learning to work in the local environment. Just as important, that approach allows for experimenting to find out what model of involvement works best—lending, equity investing, or some hybrid. Once local experience has been accumulated, only then should the larger "green fields"—new projects—be considered, and then always based on solid technical review. A corollary lesson is to buttress an inexperienced staff with veterans who know the business. They could be placed on investment committees or on boards of management. Uncle Sam loaded the boards of directors of his Enterprise Funds with volunteer, retired professionals from venture capital and other industries. Their presence helped to flatten the green staff's learning curve.

Venture investing cannot be done cheaply, using a staff paid only in salary. Those looking after the investments must have a stake in the results. The business norm is to share with managers at least 20 percent of gains from investment sales. But ADELA's program was, to quote one whistle-blower, "to pay as little as it can get away with." A senior international banker, who, in the late 1960s was Citibank's corporate head in Lima, Peru, where ADELA's main office was installed, presciently told me: "They .... seemed to be paid a lot less than we and other major bank junior officers, but they seemed to want to have the same lifestyle, a source, I suspect, for future frustrations and stretching for projects to bolster their performance."

ADELA did develop a bonus plan. But it didn't go far enough down the ranks and wasn't based on sharing the profits on the sale of investments. It favored the four senior managing directors, and it was based on "reported" profits on operations. Thus, to boost profits, stock dividends would be taken into the earnings as if they had been received in cash; and interest on delinquent loans would continue to be accrued and added to ADELA's earnings, even though uncollected and, as it turned out, uncollectible. Sharing in the actual results of investment sales would have removed the incentive to manipulate the numbers, and could have aligned owners' and staff interests. Such an incentive program would be more likely to discourage excessive risk-taking while rewarding reasonable risk-taking.

ADELA had a manual of policy and procedures for equity investing (increasingly ignored as it may have been), but it had no manual for the commercial lending function that came to be its main business. A far-extended operation needs operating manuals, strong controls, and a good internal audit system that connects right to the board. That is how management stays on top of things and how the board oversees the management. Also, under this arrangement, it is more likely that the company's statements will represent its true condition to the owners.

We can also learn important lessons from ADELA's financing practices. First, the company was highly leveraged for the kind of business it was in. For every dollar of capital the company had, it borrowed four dollars and invested in projects that were unlikely to mature within the time frame of the loan—shades of the credit squeeze in 2007 when financial giants in America (Bear Stearns) and Europe (BNP Paribas) were staggered by huge losses as a result of imprudently financing long-term real estate investments with short-term debt.

Second, in mid-course ADELA began borrowing from the market—from financial institutions that were not ADELA shareholders. They did a bit of this under Keller, but went full-throttle under his successor Gonzalez. He also did ADELA's first public borrowing—a bond issue in German marks, which came back to haunt ADELA when it had to be restructured. Much of this funding was short-to medium-term, but went into loans and investments that became long term, causing a cash squeeze down the road. The lesson is about the vital need to match the maturities of borrowings with those of the loans to which they are applied.

The larger lesson is that when ADELA went outside its base of financial shareholders to secure additional funding, it surrendered the flexibility that a venture investing company needs to remedy the inevitable difficult situations that arise later. Outside lenders bound ADELA into a straightjacket that hindered them when economic conditions turned down. Those lenders already had long lists of loans to Latin America that weren't being paid on time. They were in no mood for more of the same from ADELA. They had hedged those loans to ADELA with the bet that, in extremis, ADELA's wealthy shareholder parents would come to its rescue. When they did not, the lenders became righteously vengeful.

Risk and other management practices

A former boss at Citibank used to remind us that we were in the pure and simple business of managing financial risk. There was nothing wrong with this four letter word, he argued, as long as it was managed. (Ironically, a generation later, the U.S. Treasury had to bail out Citi when it was accused of mismanaging its business.) But ADELA indiscriminately heaped onto its pile of assets risks of all assortments without having the capacity for managing them, or even taking the time to understand them. It took on huge commercial risk, as when it went alone into real estate and agricultural development. It added credit risk when it lent to businesses and political risk when it invested in any of the twenty-plus nations of the Americas. It assumed exchange risk when it lent to Brazilian companies dollars that had to be converted into *cruzeiros*, which were often devalued daily, and then convert them back to dollars to pay the installments; or when it lent dollars to borrowers who paid back in local currency that remained frozen within the country for months and sometimes years, while being subject to devaluation.

Taking risks to achieve its mission was what ADELA was all about. But taking the right risks was the key. ADELA's owners should have reached an understanding with management as to what those risks should be, which types and levels they were comfortable with, and how they could mitigate the risks. CEO Keller did all this in the early days, but less and less effectively as ADELA expanded and diversified. Risk management required ADELA's board to set the overall parameters and then to regularly monitor ADELA's management of the risk environment to assure that the right strategies and controls were in place. They should not have left risk taking and risk management to ADELA's investment officers in the field.

Broader lessons about governance and more

For the Western world's capitalists wanting to apply development models to the African continent and beyond, and perhaps for directors in general, this may be one occasion when history provides good instruction. We may abstract some principles from the ADELA experience.

About business alliances: When businesses ally in a project, they must demand the same clarity about why they are doing it and what they expect to get out of it as when they go into a new business with their own companies. The project must develop a coherent strategy for success that utilizes what the partners bring to the project. Moreover, where each owns only a small part, the project must have an owner—an authority responsible for setting the compass and controlling the mission. What is everybody's turns out to be nobody's when things go awry.

Participating with other corporations in collective do-good endeavors that are not expected to impact the bottom line can end up being very costly. IBM, Exxon, and Dresdner Bank each wrote off $1 million (share purchase of $500,000 plus a similar contribution of capital under the restructuring agreement with the banks). But this loss was less significant than the executive time each had to devote to winding down ADELA. And there is no tallying the effect that their willingness to let ADELA fail had on the attitudes toward international business of people in government and elsewhere, in Latin America and beyond.

As to governance, when corporations go into a business that they know conceivably nothing about, they must bring overseers who do know something and who will contribute the necessary time and effort. They cannot run the business like an association, where management is left to a few professionals and board meetings are largely social events. ADELA was an alliance of powerful companies joining in a business that needed their substantial resource base and more to succeed in its serious purpose. It needed people who knew about venture investing and about doing business in Latin America, for this was to be venturing at its gamiest in a less-developed part of their world. It needed directors who actively directed. Had ADELA adopted a board-of-management style, as the Europeans were accustomed to doing, it could have opened that board to professionals experienced in the particular business, such as, for example, retired venture capitalists and other professionals with the time and the capacity to dedicate to the business. Even in ADELA's time, the use of professional directors was not a novelty.

If those who govern have a single overriding responsibility, it is to vigilantly and accountably provide for enterprise continuity. How else to act fairly toward all the constituents served—employees, customers, creditors, shareholders, communities, and governments? That a group of corporate heads could get together at the Bohemian Grove (a private men's club in San Francisco that in mid-July each year hosts a two-week encampment of some of the world's most powerful men) and think they were seeing to ADELA's well-being, demonstrates economist Paul Krugman's contention that "Bad ideas flourish because they are in the interest of powerful groups." It cannot be said that ADELA's governors and board faced up to their responsibility to manage the company.

Unlike the firms mentioned in Jim Collins's *Built to Last,* and unlike another long-lasting, ever-reinventing-itself group The Grateful Dead, ADELA remained stuck in molds unlikely to carry them through difficult times: a board that was inappropriately sized and poorly manned for the business they were in and an investment strategy that featured multiple new ventures in which the company took minority positions long after this model proved unfit. The ADELA model was not built to last.

A board of directors cannot afford to be distant from management in the field. Board members must go out to the field, not to attend banquets in capital cities, but to go with staff to visit plant sites. They must see for themselves what each is like. And a board needs a feedback mechanism that tells them how the company is doing and that challenges plans and programs. ADELA's failure demonstrates the ultimate necessity of checks and balances provided by a vigilant, accountable board of directors working through its committees.

"In the development of a successful enterprise," wrote Prof. C. Northcote Parkinson, "there must be a single-minded pursuit of profit. Bring in some other motive, admirable though it may be in itself.... The wish to bring prosperity to a poor district.... and our whole effort has from the outset a probably fatal defect." The lesson from ADELA is not that corporations cannot do well doing good but that they must do well to do good. ADELA had to be run as a competitive business to do the good it was supposed to achieve. A profitable company builds capital to sustain its growth. A losing one has its capital eroded and then declines.

This chapter began with Tesler & Cloherty's conclusion that telling ADELA's story would fail to add much value. Indeed, according to Hegel, in *Philosophy of History*, "People and governments never have learned anything from history or acted on principles deduced from it." But perhaps he meant that we do not learn, not that we cannot. I believe that the study of ADELA's failure offers useful instructions for plotting the course of new investment ventures. In a larger sense, this cautionary tale may help society avoid the deadly social and economic costs of future ADELAs, Enrons, and Tycos, as well as avert the heavy hand of a Sarbanes-Oxley.

12. Epilogue

Foreign aid comes in two models: capitalist-led and state-led. Both models have produced major disappointments. In Latin America it was true of the government-sponsored Alliance for Progress, which faded away. It was also true of ADELA's shareholders who bought their shares and put them away. According to former World Bank economist William Easterly, the tragedy is not that aid hasn't worked, but that we haven't really cared.

Addendum 1

ADELA Timeline

The curve represents the amount of ADELA's borrowing from banks

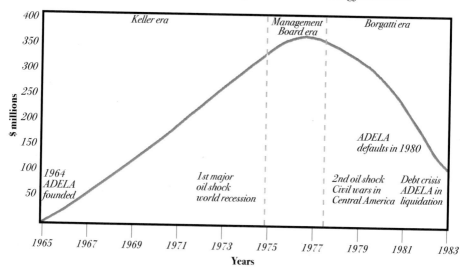

Addendum 2

><

Letter from Ernst Keller

VOLKART BROTHERS HOLDING LTD.
Winterthur, 6th June 1980
Ke/H

Mr. Joseph J. Borgatti
President
Adela Investment Company S.A.
375 Park Avenue
NEW YORK, N.Y. 10022 USA

Dear Joe,

On receipt of your letter of May 1 and the subscription offer of same date we have at VOLKART subscribed to our shares and made payment to the trustee. However, we have made the release of this payment subject to our own judgment that certain conditions have been satisfied so as to provide ADELA with a reasonable chance to survive and resume its development work in Latin America.

Why should Adela be rescued ?

In our view there only is one valid argument for rescuing Adela from its present troubles : to restore it to previous health and vigor and have it continue meeting the purpose and objectives it was originally set up for. This is our sole reason for participating in your plan.

The other two arguments we have heard, that of preventing damage to the image and reputation of private enterprise, foreign investors and of the shareholders of Adela, and that of injecting substantial fresh capital only for gaining time for an orderly liquidation are, in our view, not valid. An orderly liquidation can be decided by the creditors without an infusion of fresh capital. In a liquidation all fresh capital now being sought from the shareholders would be lost. It would mean to ask the shareholders to throw good money after bad.

The damage to the image and reputation of private enterprise and of the shareholders has largely been done. Liquidation or bankruptcy would make it worse, but only slightly. To Latin Americans and to the financial communities the image of Adela's shareholders would look worse, if they now inject a substantial amount of fresh capital without results, if this money only buys some time and Adela fails a year or two later.

In Latin America Adela has over the past few years become increasingly inactive, invisible, no longer present and represented in the right places by the right people. it has liquidated most of its good investments and some other assets at almost any price, first to show a record profit in 1977 (nearly all derived from realization of hidden reserves) and later to forestall insolvency. of late it has been unable to make new commitments or even meet disbursements on investments and loans. In the international financial markets Adela's previously solid reputation as a respected borrower has been shattered. There is little to salvage on image and reputation, they have to be built from below zero. The only way to achieve this and to also repair the damage done by these recent developments to the reputation of the shareholders is to rebuild the company, restore it to its previous health and activity, bring it back to where it can again be useful to Latin America and reasonably profitable.

Is the Adela concept viable?

This question seems to be raised again lately, in view of the company's present difficult situation. The same question was around in the preincorporation era in 1963/64 but then disappeared during 1965, the company's first year of operation and was not heard any more for more than a decade. It would seem absurd to question the viability of a company with the performance of Adela during more than a decade through 1975, specifically its role and effectiveness as a developer of private enterprise in Latin America which, measured against its own limited resources, has far exceeded that of comparable organizations, private or public its own steady development from 1964 through 1975, in terms of paidin capital ($ 16 m. at incorporation to $ 62 m.), total assets (to $ 450 m.) and earnings ($ 1.1 m. in 1966, the first full year to $ 6.5 m. in 1975, after taxes and losswrite offs); and its solid financial situation and high liquidity built over the years, reflected accumulated open surplus and reserves of $ 32 m. plus hidden reserves of equal magnitude (in form of realizable capital gains), making for total surplus and reserves in excess of its total equity holdings or total paidin capital.

The viability of a company with this record of meeting its stated objectives, contributing to development at a profit, is hardly debatable. More appropriate questions would be After Adela proved viable over more than a decade, what are the causes of its present dismal situation ? What has gone wrong and why ?

The answer to these questions is quite simple but unpleasant. The company has been dismantled and destroyed, from some of its fundamental policies and operating procedures over its organization and its fine team of officers and professionals, to its capacity and ability to operate and, as an inevitable consequence, its solid financial situation and high solvency. An exodus of nearly all of its officers and professionals has left the company incapacitated for taking advantage of opportunities and, more serious, managing its assets and liabilities. Most of Adela's present predicament of a huge amount of non-income producing assets accumulated over some years is attributable to neglect of asset management. Control instruments for monitoring investments and loans were ignored, the part of the organization dedicated to monitoring, auditing and management of investments and for coping with problems was dismantled or allowed to disintegrate with nothing replacing it. The officers and professionals engaged in these vital functions, the talent most difficult to find and train, all left the company in short order. With their departure Adela lost all capacity and capabilities for performing services which are indispensable for venture capital activities in developing countries. Somewhat later the team at the Zurich office, engaged in procuring funds, providing liability management and management information services also was dismantled and left.

Page 19 of Section III of the subscription offer of May 1 provides an illustration of the effects of dismantling or losing the vital investment monitoring and management services. It lists 7 investments with a total exposure of $48 million, representing about one third present non income producing assets. These investments were on the books in 1975, but with only one third of the present exposure, a total of $16 million. Two of them were profitable and paid dividends, two others were in an early development stage and two were red listed as problem cases, one of them en route to recovery. What is now at $10.3 million the largest of the seven, Paraty/Trindade in Brazil, was $1.1 million, one tenth, in 1975, with a ban put on additional commitments to this project due to its sensitivity to the then evident energy problems. In most of these projects exposures multiplied but problems, in some cases existing, in others ensuing, remained unsolved because more money alone will not do. And with its investment management services gone Adela no longer was capable of providing the essential input for turnarounds management assistance. It is not uncommon that policies and operating procedures change when after considerable time there is a change at the top of a company. It is the privilege of every new chief executive to organize his company along the lines he deems best suited for achieving its objectives. However, we know of no other case where all of a company's intangible assets, knowledge and experience acquired over a decade, proven policies and operating procedures, and a well running organization have been as completely thrown overboard as in Adela, with nothing to replace it. Nor do we know of any organization which could still hope to run its business after changing chief executives four times in that many years and losing 95% of its most valuable asset, its officers and professionals. Adela's failure in the past few years and its present dismal situation have nothing to do with the viability of its concept, nor with the changing environment and market in Latin America. The company's predicament is all man made. It can be corrected, but this will take considerably longer than projected. It will be far more difficult to rebuild Adela than to build it from scratch. The restoration plan A restoration plan was presented previously on March 12 and again, in a modified version, on May 1. We have a few comments and questions on some aspects of the plan.

1) Financial restructuring: Though in the latest plan the term over which you hope to recover a major portion of presently non income producing assets has been extended, we believe it to be still far too optimistic. We note that in the latest plan you expect only $40 million of fresh equity capital. We feel that the initially projected amount of $50 million

may have been "too little, too late" and believe anything less will not do. As to the debt consolidation we feel that every attempt should be made to further extend the repayment term, beyond the one year grace and five years of quarterly instalments now planned. A slower recovery of assets will require a longer term, as otherwise newly injected equity capital will have to be used for debt repayment. We would consider this unacceptable. In this connection we note that you plan to hold the newly subscribed funds from shareholders on term deposit for two years, until June 30, 1982. Is this the best way of employing this new capital ? Or is this thought as a cash reserve for meeting debt repayments ?

2) Management: We note that the previously mentioned Management Committee should now have no line authority, but purely advisory and informative functions. While we would prefer this watered down role of this committee over the previous version we continue to question the need and wisdom of "management by committee". Firstly, any emergency requires clear and ample authority for taking decisions, and Adela's present situation is without doubt an emergency. Secondly, even in previous more normal times Adela needed "hands on management" in the places where its opportunities and problems were. Both the nature of its business and Adela's present situation do not allow for management from an executive suite, and much less for management by committee. Any such committee, whether advisory or supervisory, is in our view undesirable and an additional hindrance for an already most difficult task. It would tend to blur responsibility and authority which must clearly be yours. We also doubt whether the shareholders, creditors and IFC are prepared to make some of their highest caliber men available for any length of time, as the situation would require. And a group of frightened "funcionarios" trying to exercise a decisive influence on management and activities could easily be the kiss of death.

160

3) Organization There is no indication in the plan as to the organization structure which you visualize for achieving the turn around. It has been rather widely recognized that Adela seems to have a strange structure at this time, with many share holders not exactly knowing where it is. Lima, still the most viable location from geographical, legal and cost viewpoints, was abandoned as headquarters (as "too luxurious") and moved to Park Avenue in New York (less luxurious ?, less costly ?). But New York seems to have assumed more the role of the previous Zurich office than of the Lima operations center. Where do you plan to headquarter the company ? For some time to come little new business can be done. The main task at hand is to recover money and pay off debt. For this you will need capable people stationed where the problems are, but not a whole network of offices as was justified for doing several hundred million dollars' worth of new business each year. Except for the trouble shooters stationed in the field the organization could be small and should be centralized in a place with easy access to Latin America, preferably in Latin America. Shareholders: Adela probably has the most prominent ownership of any company, a great asset in the fair weather era 1964-1975. But Adela has no real owners, and this is a grave disadvantage in difficult times as you are now passing through. A concentration of ownership would be desirable. If not achievable now it should be envisaged in the future, at a time when you begin to see light on the horizon on your restoration plan but need further capital for doing new business. What Adela seems to be short of most at this juncture is the strong personal commitment and support from a number of business leaders as I had in the incipient years. Could such support be mobilized again ? It would be invaluable.

One of the causes mentioned for the deterioration of Adela's situation in past years was a change of the market for its services, specifically greater competition by a considerably larger number of banks, international and domestic. Adela's markets in Latin America have always been subject to changes, some of them unexpected and radical, caused by political events and major economic shifts. However, competition from banks never presented a problem, despite the growing influx of banking activities over the years, as a consequence of greater political stability, a more favourable investment environment and above average economic growth in the majority of Latin American countries. Adela's services were from the outset of its activities planned to be complementary to those of banks. Banks do not invest in equity, and international banks without branch operations in Latin America can with all their greater aggressiveness in seeking business not lend to medium size or even larger private enterprises. There is and always was competition in this market by domestic banks, but in most countries their funding is insufficient and does not allow them to engage in a great deal of medium term lending. This has not materially changed. For its venture capital activity the opportunities available in Latin America continue to far exceed the capacity of a restored Adela plus that of several similar institutions. On lending activities competition has increased but not Much in the sector of medium size enterprises which always was Adela's major field. While it is annoying to lose borrowers to shareholder banks when they become internationally bankable, this was always the case, is in fact part of Adela's function as a catalyst for investment. Finally, there are virtually limitless opportunities for the kind of development services Adela used to provide (essentially identification, development and implementation of projects). As a whole the environment for private enterprise and for foreign investment has vastly improved over the late sixties/early seventies. There are always dangers and risks, such as presently high rates of inflation, usually coupled with more frequent devaluation of currencies and, of course, high cost of money, domestically and internationally. High money cost can make new projects economically marginal or unfeasible and can get existing enterprises into financial trouble. But Adela's activity by nature is risky and the company's success was always dependent on the management's willingness and ability to cope with problems. It would be a fatal error to assume that Adela in the future would not encounter just as many problems as in its past, if it wants to meet the objectives it was set up for. One way of making the Adela concept unviable would be to turn it into a company unwilling to take risks and running from problems instead of coping with them. You are undoubtedly receiving a lot of unsolicited advice these days, thus you may consider ours worth what it has cost you, which is nothing. We hope that your restoration plan can get under way soon and we wish you the best of luck and success.

Sincrely yours,
Volkart Brothers Holding, Ltd.
Ernst Keller, Chairman

Addendum 3

>∽

BAEF: The AMETA case

This is about an investment by the BAEF in AMETA, a chicken and egg producer in Bulgaria. When the investment soured, the CEO brought it to the board. Then one of the directors, knowledgeable in the business, took the lead to help the BAEF deal with the company's problems and at the same time build the board's comprehension.

AMETA is a vertically-integrated poultry producer in Bulgaria in which the BAEF had made an investment. In the late 1990s the BAEF's CEO told the board that AMETA was becoming a $6 million problem investment. The slaughter house was badly in need of repair; operating performance was below standard; management was weak; financial losses were large and increasing; and there were problems with feed. As a result, he had removed the Manager and replaced him as a stop-gap measure with a young investment manager from the BAEF. One of the directors of BAEF, a partner in an agricultural consulting company based in Washington, D.C., became directly involved in the company's situation and began making regular visits to the plant. That was no easy hop as the plant was located in an interior region of Bulgaria, seven time zones away from Washington. The director led an evaluation of the company and, most important, provided reassurance to the Board about the company's situation that made it comfortable in putting more money in to save the company. In addition to assisting the CEO of the BAEF in implementing the rehabilitation and modernization of the company, he sought and found a manager (located in the U.S.) with the skills and experience to complement the BAEF investment manager. Five years later, AMETA had annual sales of $30 million, was hugely profitable, current on its loans from BAEF, and had paid down over $1 million on them, thus reducing BAEF's exposure to $5 million. The latest development is that all the loans have been repaid, and BAEF has sold the firm to the two men. After their final payment in September 2011, BAEF reported a gain of $6 million on an investment that had been a potential $7 million loss. AMETA has now some 1,300 employees selling over EUR 100 million per year. It has become the gold standard of chicken and egg production in Bulgaria.

"As I reflect on the AMETA experience," said the director who had stepped forward to save the investment, "our principal strengths were in having a management that didn't attempt to hide the problem, and a group of directors who were willing to get directly involved to help solve problems when their experience was relevant." The directors' active participation in the resolution of this problem investment was not unusual in the BAEF.

About the author

>━━

Joe Borgatti was born in 1923 of Italian immigrants in Somerville, Massachusetts. He attended the public schools of that city and then was accepted to Harvard College. Finding, after a few months, that he could not fulfill the calculus requirement, he left school and, as World War II had commenced, joined the US Army. He served for three and one half years with the US Air Force as a tail gunner with a bombing squadron in the South Pacific Theater, and was discharged in late 1945. He promptly reapplied to Harvard, was accepted in 1946, and graduated in a little over three years. As an undergraduate he managed the Harvard University Band, and that experience helped him win admission to Harvard Business School where he graduated "With Distinction" in 1951. Joe's long professional career of 66 years, most of it outside the U.S. in countries as diverse as Brazil, Bulgaria, Egypt and Guatemala, includes four different specialties: banking, nickel mining-refining, venture investing and privatization. Joe breaks down his years as follows:

Growing up-fm 1923 to 1941	18 years
Military service & higher education	10 years
Professional life - mostly abroad	66 years
Current age	94

Joe regards his 20-year association with the hugely successful Bulgarian-American Enterprise Fund, and its legatee, the America for Bulgaria Foundation, as being involved with a group that was doing development right.